Constitutional Inequality

GILBERT Y. STEINER

Constitutional Inequality
The Political Fortunes of the
Equal Rights Amendment

THE BROOKINGS INSTITUTION
Washington, D.C.

Library of Congress Cataloging in Publication data:

Steiner, Gilbert Yale, 1924–
   Constitutional inequality.

   Includes bibliographical references and index.
1. Equal rights amendments—United States. I. Title.
KF4758.S73   1985   342.73′085   84-45854
                       347.30285
ISBN 0-8157-8128-8
ISBN 0-8157-8127-X (pbk.)

1 2 3 4 5 6 7 8 9

THE BROOKINGS INSTITUTION is an independent organization devoted to nonpartisan research, education, and publication in economics, government, foreign policy, and the social sciences generally. Its principal purposes are to aid in the development of sound public policies and to promote public understanding of issues of national importance.

The Institution was founded on December 8, 1927, to merge the activities of the Institute for Government Research, founded in 1916, the Institute of Economics, founded in 1922, and the Robert Brookings Graduate School of Economics and Government, founded in 1924.

The Board of Trustees is responsible for the general administration of the Institution, while the immediate direction of the policies, program, and staff is vested in the President, assisted by an advisory committee of the officers and staff. The by-laws of the Institution state: "It is the function of the Trustees to make possible the conduct of scientific research, and publication, under the most favorable conditions, and to safeguard the independence of the research staff in the pursuit of their studies and in the publication of the results of such studies. It is not a part of their function to determine, control, or influence the conduct of particular investigations or the conclusions reached."

The President bears final responsibility for the decision to publish a manuscript as a Brookings book. In reaching his judgment on the competence, accuracy, and objectivity of each study, the President is advised by the director of the appropriate research program and weighs the views of a panel of expert outside readers who report to him in confidence on the quality of the work. Publication of a work signifies that it is deemed a competent treatment worthy of public consideration but does not imply endorsement of conclusions or recommendations.

The Institution maintains its position of neutrality on issues of public policy in order to safeguard the intellectual freedom of the staff. Hence interpretations or conclusions in Brookings publications should be understood to be solely those of the authors and should not be attributed to the Institution, to its trustees, officers, or other staff members, or to the organizations that support its research.

Foreword

THIS BOOK simultaneously addresses the subject of women's rights and the process of constitutional change. It is neither a psychological nor a sociological treatise on the women's movement, but rather focuses on the complexities of accomplishing substantive policy change by constitutional amendment. The author examines the effects of institutions, laws, rules, lobbying strategies, and timing on the outcomes of fights over the equal rights amendment from its halcyon days in 1971-72 to its subsequent dark days when the proposal failed to win ratification in the states and then failed to win renewal in Congress.

Unpersuaded by a review of common post hoc explanations for the loss of the ERA, Gilbert Y. Steiner looks to circumstances not present during congressional consideration or during the initial wave of ratifications. He finds that the window of opportunity for passage and ratification opened widest in the brief period between organized labor's reconsideration of protective legislation for women and the Supreme Court's decriminalization of abortion. Unrelated chance factors—legislative absenteeism, the timing of state legislative sessions, state constitutional change—first hampered prompt access to the window. Thereafter, the window successively lowered as the ERA's leading congressional critic acquired the status of "savior of the Constitution" at the Watergate hearings, the abortion dispute became increasingly heated, and the Soviet invasion of Afghanistan gave the possible conscription of women a chilling new dimension. Nevertheless, ratification failed by only a handful of votes. Proponents subsequently resorted to legislative shortcuts in an effort to revive the ERA. But employing such strategems in connection with an amendment to the Constitution produced a backlash that was more costly than beneficial.

From all of this, Steiner deduces a critical link between the controversies over abortion and the ERA. Formal constitutional change to adopt an ERA requires a measure of consensus that the abortion dispute now makes impossible. The book concludes with an analysis of available alternatives, and a proposal for future strategy that, while controversial, would combine good government and good politics.

Gilbert Y. Steiner is a senior fellow in the Governmental Studies program of the Brookings Institution. His previous Brookings books deal with the politics of welfare, children's, and family policy.

The author gratefully acknowledges thoughtful comments on this manuscript from Janet K. Boles, Anne N. Costain, Jo Freeman, Cynthia E. Harrison, Andrew S. McFarland, Jane Mansbridge, and Paul E. Peterson. The manuscript was edited by Alice M. Carroll and processed for publication by Julie J. Bailes. Diana Regenthal prepared the index.

The views expressed here are those of the author and should not be ascribed to the trustees, officers, or other staff members of the Brookings Institution.

BRUCE K. MACLAURY
President

March 1985
Washington, D.C.

Contents

Chapter One

The Rejection of
Constitutional Equality

AN OPPRESSED MAJORITY in a democratic system is a political paradox that admits of no ready explanation. Women are a majority of the United States population, live longer than men—thereby magnifying their majority among persons of voting age—and vote in greater numbers than men. In the 1984 national election, eligible female voters outnumbered eligible male voters by eight million. Women also organize politically, campaign, and lobby. Conventional appreciation of the way a democratic system functions would deem it improbable for a group of this size and these behavioral characteristics to be denied a formal guarantee of equal rights comparable to that accorded racial minorities and immigrants. Improbable or not, a constitutional guarantee has been denied repeatedly—first by congressional inaction; then, while the Supreme Court insisted on judicial restraint, by failure of the requisite number of states to ratify favorable congressional action; and, subsequently, by unfavorable congressional action.

Had it been adopted, the equal rights amendment (ERA) would have resolved the paradox by adding to the Constitution a provision that "Equality of rights under the law shall not be denied or abridged by the United States or by any state on account of sex." But ten years and three months after its overwhelming approval by Congress, the proposed amendment died, three states shy of the thirty-eight needed to ratify. Brought de novo to the floor of the House of Representatives seventeen months later, the ERA failed by six votes to secure the required two-thirds majority. If, during much of the period of congressional inaction, women's groups and their allies were barely visible and little heard, the later state and federal rejections came in the face of a well-organized movement for women's rights.

The women's cause has not rejected alternative paths to constitu-

1

tional equality. It does insist, however, that any alternative path be as broad and as clear of debris as is the proposed constitutional amendment. If the Supreme Court can clear such a path, it has chosen not to do so. At one point the Court did come within one vote of declaring sex a "suspect classification" only to back away when Justice Lewis Powell declined to provide the needed vote, with the observation that the issue was even then out to the states for resolution—an inhibition an earlier Court had not felt in effectively striking down child labor.[1] As for the statutory path, Representative Ken Kramer, a Colorado Republican, has proposed a women's equal rights act, a kind of congressional memorandum to the Supreme Court declaring sex a suspect classification entitled to the coverage of the Fourteenth Amendment's equal protection clause.[2] But because of his simultaneous opposition to a constitutional amendment to that effect, and the Court's earlier unwillingness to act without one, Kramer's proposal smacks of an effort to have it both ways.

Inequality Sustained

Denial of equal rights for women once found its justification in a policy of special or compensatory protection for a presumably weaker sex. As more women perceived compensatory protection to be a smokescreen for economic inequality, an increasing number of women's groups sought to abandon protection in favor of legal equality. Others, especially labor union women, continued to believe the loss of protective legislation would weaken their position and that of their low-income sisters. Politicians sympathetic to the latter view insisted that any equal rights proposal be qualified to preserve "rights, benefits, or exemptions conferred by law" on women.[3]

1. *United States* v. *Darby,* 312 U.S. 100 (1941). When the *Darby* decision made it unnecessary, a proposed child labor amendment had been ratified by twenty-eight states, eight shy of the required three-fourths.
2. H. R. 1131, 98 Cong. 1 sess. The bill would prohibit any government from making or enforcing by law a classification based on gender unless such classification were "necessary to achieve a compelling government interest and is the least burdensome alternative possible." See also Gayle Binion, "The Case for an Equal Rights Act," *Center Magazine,* vol. 16 (November–December 1983), pp. 2–7.
3. *Congressional Record,* vol. 96 (1950), pp. 861–71. "Between 1945 and 1960, the proponents of the ERA and the defenders of protective labor legislation would not reconcile their views, based as they were in opposite philosophies of women's needs."

The united opposition of organized labor and its liberal friends for years deterred Congress from proposing an unqualified equal rights amendment to the Constitution. To neither side's particular satisfaction, a resolution qualified with a protection proviso passed the Senate as early as 1950. Just short of two decades later, the United Auto Workers determined protective legislation to be "a millstone around the neck of women at work," and labor opposition slowly began to reverse itself.[4] The reversal evolved too slowly to influence views on constitutional protection of equal rights for women held by Emanuel Celler, a liberal New York Democrat who, as chairman of the House of Representatives Judiciary Committee, had grown accustomed to foreclosing the proposed amendment from House consideration. But it emboldened others to challenge him. Celler was eventually finessed—by a woman colleague, Martha Griffiths, Democrat of Michigan, who used a discharge petition to achieve a vote on the House floor.

Favorable congressional action followed easily. A constitutional amendment passed the House in 1971 and the Senate in 1972. Sponsors thought it inconceivable that the proposal might fail to be ratified by the states subsequent to its success in Congress. "This amendment, if passed," said Representative Griffiths in 1971, "would be ratified in less than two years."[5] Her confidence seemed not unreasonable.

When the requisite thirty-eight states failed to ratify it by June 30, 1982, however, the equal rights amendment became the first proposed amendment in post-Civil War constitutional history formally to expire after congressional passage. (The child labor amendment, proposed in 1924 without a deadline for ratification, remains in legal

---

Cynthia E. Harrison, "Prelude to Feminism: Women's Organizations, the Federal Government and the Rise of the Women's Movement, 1942 to 1968" (Ph.D. dissertation, Columbia University, 1982), p. 131.

4. "Statement of Stephen Schlossberg, General Counsel, International Union, UAW, to the Equal Employment Opportunity Commission," Washington, D.C., May 2, 1967, p. 5. See also Walter P. Reuther, "Administrative Letter to All Local Unions," November 6, 1969. The UAW convention of April 1970 formally adopted a resolution favoring the equal rights amendment. The AFL-CIO would not follow suit until its 1973 convention.

5. *Equal Rights for Men and Women, 1971,* Hearings before Subcommittee No. 4 of the House Judiciary Committee , 92 Cong. 1 sess. (Government Printing Office, 1971), p. 41.

limbo although de facto dead.) That unwelcome distinction would have come to the ERA earlier save for Congress's willingness in 1979 to add thirty-nine months to the time originally allowed for ratification. The extension of time—itself unprecedented if only because no other proposal carrying a time limit for ratification had needed an extension—added to the ignominy as the thirty-nine months of grace mirrored the previous twenty-six months. No state ratified the amendment in either period.

Supporters in and out of Congress insist that the equal rights amendment will be neither abandoned nor compromised, but sustained until successful. For example, Senator Ernest F. Hollings, Democrat of South Carolina, whose state did not ratify, quoted with approval South Carolina's ERA leader who wrote him, "We shall not give up." A day after the ratification deadline expired, Senator Bob Packwood rallied the troops. "Today is the beginning of a new era," proclaimed the Oregon Republican. "There is no substitute for ERA. And there is no excuse for its failure."[6]

A number of congressional supporters who believe opponents transgressed the implicit rules of politics are too angry to take the loss of the ERA philosophically. They characterize the strategies and tactics of opposition groups as misrepresentations or worse—a "barrage of misinformation and lies. . . falsehoods and distortions"; "procedural machinations"; "they distorted. . . they lied"; "hysterical accusation, exaggeration, and even outright fabrication." Bob Packwood's complaints extend to what he regards as a lack of taste in the opposition's victory celebration. "When we win—and we will win—" says Packwood, "I hope that when we celebrate our victory we will celebrate it with grace and dignity and forgiveness."[7] Unhappily, those virtues were in short supply on both sides at the end of the ten-year campaign for ratification.

House and Senate sponsors wasted no time before reviving the cause. One hundred and fifty of the former and forty-five of the latter indicated on July 1, 1982, that they intended to cosponsor another ERA. Many appeared willing to vote on the spot. But Senator Nancy Kassebaum, Republican of Kansas, believes that a rational review of the failed effort should be undertaken before the campaign for an

6. *Congressional Record,* daily edition (July 1, 1982), pp. S7771–72.
7. Ibid.

ERA is resumed. Kassebaum finds no inconsistency in her support of the amendment and her low opinion of the quality of the equal rights debate, "an area in which we must clearly seek improvement." She thinks it sensible carefully to reexamine the concerns of those who objected to the proposed amendment. "We need to take this opportunity to determine what went wrong and how to correct it."[8]

Kassebaum's judgment seems not to be widely shared. A Senate sponsor, unprepared to answer substantive questions about the amendment at a 1983 hearing, gave short shrift to the concerns of the opposition. So did leaders of the House of Representatives who decided to try to move the ERA through that chamber under a suspension of the rules procedure just before adjourning the 1983 session. Rather than provide opponents an opportunity to air their concerns and offer amendments, the decision was to limit debate and bar any effort to change the language adopted in 1972. When a dozen House members who were cosponsors of the ERA pronounced the procedure unfair or unwarranted, and voted no, the resolution failed (278–147) to win the required two-thirds majority. As a consequence, proponents remain unable to achieve constitutional assurance that "equality of rights under the law shall not be denied or abridged by the United States or by any state on account of sex."

Three Generations or More?

Some legislators and some leaders of women's groups find comfort in likening the slow pace of the ERA effort to that of the fight for woman suffrage. "It took three generations of women to obtain the basic, fundamental, democratic right to vote," Senator George Mitchell, Democrat of Maine, says. "Perhaps it will take another three generations of women to obtain equal protection under the supreme law of our land."[9] Mitchell's philosophic outlook, no doubt meant to cheer ERA partisans, implies that the ultimately successful fight for woman suffrage had a significantly longer history than the fight for an equal rights amendment has had.

A closer examination of Mitchell's hypothesis is more likely to chill

8. Ibid., p. S7787.
9. Ibid. (July 14, 1982), p. S8177.

than to cheer ERA partisans. For the suffrage movement, the three generations before its success started with the Seneca Falls Woman's Rights Convention of 1848 and ended with ratification of the Nineteenth Amendment in 1920. The beginning of the equal rights drive is commonly dated from the first introduction in Congress of an amendment in 1923. Three generations comparable to those of the suffrage movement would give the ERA until the mid-1990s to achieve constitutional status. However, there may be as persuasive a case for the Seneca Falls meeting as the beginning of the equal rights idea as for that of woman suffrage. The suffrage resolution hardly dominated Seneca Falls. As Eleanor Flexner notes in her classic history of the women's rights movement, suffrage carried at Seneca Falls by only a small margin, and it was the only resolution not unanimously agreed to. Although no separate resolution on equal rights was offered, a third of the three hundred participants signed a Declaration of Principles asserting equality of the sexes: "We hold these truths to be self-evident: that all men and women are created equal; that they are endowed by their Creator with certain inalienable rights; that among these are life, liberty and the pursuit of happiness."[10]

Neither the suffrage resolution nor the Declaration of Principles discussed the specifics of implementation—constitutional change was not mentioned. The birth dates of the equal rights cause and of the suffrage cause are equally difficult to establish. (Flexner characterizes Seneca Falls as the birth of the women's rights movement only in the sense that birth is a stage in the process of growth.) If Seneca Falls were accepted as birth date for both, and constitutional change accepted as the test of success for both, equal rights would be well into its second century without success, but suffrage would have achieved success after seventy-two years.

Another way to compare the respective gestation periods is to date each from the year of first introduction in Congress. By that standard, woman suffrage can be traced to 1868. It was passed in 1919, ratified in 1920—a period of fifty-two years from introduction to ratification. The equal rights amendment—passed by Congress in 1972—was first introduced in 1923. Fifty-two years later, there were good prospects for its matching the suffrage record. But the prospects were not realized. From original introduction to initial congressional passage,

10. *Century of Struggle* (Harvard University Press, Belknap Press, 1975), pp. 77, 75.

the ERA and woman suffrage required about the same number of years. Actual inclusion of suffrage in the Constitution was accomplished in two generations. The ERA will do well to be accomplished in three.

From Protection to Equal Opportunity

The most persistent and most compelling trouble that crippled prospects for an ERA from its introduction in 1923 until a year after Congress initially passed it on to the states was opposition from most of organized labor during a period of ascending labor strength. The conversion of the labor movement to support of the proposed amendment was not completed until the 1973 AFL-CIO convention. Organized labor then, in the manner of converts, became both holier than the saints and harshly intolerant of unbelievers.

When Senator Charles Curtis, Kansas Republican, at the behest of the National Woman's party, introduced the first proposal for an equal rights amendment in 1923, trade unionists foresaw the loss of protective labor legislation that gave special advantages—unequal, preferential rights—to women in matters of wages, hours, and working conditions. At the ensuing Senate Judiciary Committee hearings, labor union women led an eloquent group of women activists in opposition. These women believed that if the proposal meant equal rights for upper-class women, it meant less than equal rights for working-class women. "The working women are not so much concerned about property rights—they have no property," Melinda Scott, a United Textile Workers organizer is quoted as telling the senators. "The National Woman's Party does not know what it is to work 10 or 12 hours a day in a factory; so they do not know what it means to lose an eight-hour-day or a nine-hour-day law. The working women do know."[11] The National Woman's party (NWP) was outnumbered and outflanked at this February 1923 hearing by the combination of union women like Scott and Rose Schneiderman of the United Cap Workers, civic women like Mary Van Kleeck who during World War I headed the predecessor agency of the Department of Labor's

11. Philip S. Foner, *Women and the American Labor Movement* (Free Press, 1980), p. 143.

Women's Bureau, and church-related women like Agnes Reagan of the National Council of Catholic Women. The NWP group declined to testify. The ERA proposal died.

An equal rights amendment was offered in every subsequent Congress for the next five decades. Over and over again, however, it was consigned to Congress's death row, destroyed by the formidable union opposition. The latter easily beat back a weak National Woman's party, disdainfully described in 1943 by a leading scholar of constitutional development as including "most of the more vociferous personnel, the people who engaged in picketing, hunger strikes, and other melodramatic performances."[12] While this contempt for the NWP and the equal rights amendment was transmitted to a generation of students of constitutional development, the characterization of the NWP's members and their style is inaccurate. Redirected toward passage of an ERA after the success of the woman suffrage campaign, the organization's personnel were no less indefatigable than vociferous, and neither hunger strikes nor "other melodramatic performances" were part of the NWP's stock in trade.[13] At the same time, it is also unfair to characterize the supporters of protective legislation as short-sighted. For them, protective legislation was a realistic alternative to exploitation, and workplace equality an unrealistic pipe dream of the nonworking class.

Ironically, only two months after labor's initial attack on the ERA early in 1923, the Supreme Court struck down a minimum wage law for women in *Adkins* v. *Children's Hospital.*[14] Because the opinion asserted that the Nineteenth Amendment—woman suffrage—had reduced the civil inferiority of women almost to the "vanishing point," it invited doubt that other protective legislation for women could survive. Most of that legislation depended on the 1908 opinion in *Muller* v. *Oregon,* the case in which the Court—accepting as pertinent the then-novel Brandeis sociological brief — had upheld Oregon's limitation of women's working hours.[15] If the Nineteenth

12. Carl Brent Swisher, *American Constitutional Development* (Riverside Press, 1943), p. 702.

13. Sophonisba Breckinridge, *Women in the Twentieth Century* (McGraw-Hill, 1933), pp. 69–70; Carl Degler, *At Odds* (Oxford University Press, 1980), pp. 402–05; Sheila Rothman, *Woman's Proper Place* (Basic Books, 1978), pp. 157–60.

14. 261 U.S. 525 (1923).

15. 208 U.S. 412 (1908).

Amendment was to be read as having overcome women's civil inferiority, would governmental protection of women's health as well as women's wages now be unconstitutional? Any such outcome involving the loss of protective legislation would have destroyed the rationale for labor opposition to the ERA.

Had affirmation and extension of the *Adkins* decision and its judgment of the potency of the Nineteenth Amendment come to pass, trade union objections to an equal rights amendment might have ended half a century earlier than they did. Of course, an equally plausible reaction would have been continued hostility to an ERA along with a union-initiated drive for a constitutional amendment to overrule *Adkins*. In any event, labor first read *Adkins* narrowly as a District of Columbia case involving federal rather than state authority in the area of protective legislation. The narrow interpretation and the absence of a comparable state case involving either wages or hours made it possible to continue to have faith, at least for the time being, in protective labor legislation for women.

That faith was again challenged in 1936 with the decision in *Morehead* v. *Tipaldo* invalidating on authority of *Adkins* a minimum wage law for women in New York state.[16] Although maximum hours legislation, limits on weights women might lift, compulsory rest periods, and other women's health issues were not involved in *Morehead,* their future had to be judged uncertain at best in light of the stream of Supreme Court opinions of that period. Labor's case against an ERA seemed to be an incidental casualty of the Supreme Court's case against the New Deal.

The 1936 national election results emboldened President Roosevelt to take on the Court with his plan to "pack" it with an additional justice for every sitting judge over the age of seventy. The plan was denounced, but there was a discernible shift in the Court's responses. Early in 1937, *Adkins* was explicitly overruled in *West Coast Hotel Co.* v. *Parrish,* [17] thereby saving protective legislation for women and justifying the unions' continued opposition to an equal rights amendment—opposition that held firm until the United Auto Workers broke ranks and endorsed the amendment in 1970. The AFL-CIO did not follow suit until 1973. By then, Congress had already passed an

16. 298 U.S. 587 (1936).
17. 300 U.S. 379 (1937).

equal rights amendment, and the conflict over protective legislation for women had been mooted by legislative enactments stemming from the Civil Rights Act of 1964.

Through the years of the New Deal and the Truman administration, however, protective legislation for women held a firm place on organized labor's list of policy favorites. Since an ERA threatened protective laws, it and its supporters qualified as the enemy. Out of political expediency or personal conviction or both, the leaders of the Department of Labor and of its Women's Bureau took care to oppose an ERA and protect their president and party from labor's outrage. A couple of months before the 1944 election, bureau personnel master-minded organization of a National Committee to Defeat the Unequal Rights Amendment. Its members included the AFL, the CIO, other labor groups, the League of Women Voters, the YWCA, and the National Councils of Jewish, Catholic, and Negro Women, respectively. In the 1944 Democratic party platform, a perfunctory endorsement of an ERA balanced the support for it by professional and business women against the opposition of labor women and elected and appointed officials.

Opposition from the Women's Bureau first cracked—but did not break—when President Eisenhower appointed to head the bureau a former businesswoman and state legislator who had sponsored Connecticut's equal pay law. Moving initially to a neutral stance, the bureau soon seemed to heel in favor of the ERA but was snapped back to neutrality by a politically sensitive secretary of labor who preferred not to antagonize the department's putative constituency, labor. At the same time, Republican leaders, like their Democratic counterparts, considered it politic to acknowledge the interest of organized business and professional women in an ERA.

After the 1956 election, labor opponents of the ERA had reason to believe their cause was lost. The Republican platform had again endorsed an ERA, and Eisenhower had included an endorsement of "equality of rights" for women in a major campaign speech on civil rights and again in his budget message to Congress in January 1957.[18]

18. Republican Platform 1956, in Donald Bruce Johnson, comp., *National Party Platforms* (University of Illinois Press, 1978), p. 554; "Address in Madison Square Garden, New York City, October 25, 1956," and "Annual Budget Message to the Congress for Fiscal Year 1958," *Public Papers of the Presidents: Dwight D. Eisenhower, 1956* (GPO, 1958), p. 1020, and *1957* (GPO, 1958), p. 57.

In the end, however, there was less there than met the ear. If, as Cynthia E. Harrison observes, both the ERA's supporters and its labor opponents "believed the President to be in favor of the ERA and the Department of Labor to be opposed," they were about one-quarter right. Eisenhower, despite the speeches, really gave ERA little or no attention while the department worked at avoiding any forthright stand.

With the administration disposed either to withdraw its opposition or to waffle, organized labor alone put down the ERA in the last years of the Eisenhower administration. Harrison describes the AFL-CIO's performance: "Its Industrial Union Department urged affiliate unions to 'keep up a constant barrage of communications to members of Congress,' a campaign coordinated by legislative representative Esther Peterson. Every Senator received a letter asking him or her to vote against the dreaded Amendment. . . . Organized labor easily outweighed the influence of the National Woman's Party, whose membership had dropped throughout the decade."[19]

Esther Peterson, unlike most labor activists, supported John Kennedy for the Democratic presidential nomination in 1960 and worked on his behalf. Her subsequent reward was a joint appointment as director of the Women's Bureau and assistant secretary of labor, positions that made it easy to keep watch over and influence the struggle over an ERA versus protective legislation. At Peterson's urging, Kennedy appointed a Commission on the Status of Women that Peterson claimed would divert "troublesome" agitation about the ERA into constructive channels. From Peterson's point of view, it did. The commission found that an ERA "need not now be sought," and that protective legislation for women should be maintained, strengthened, and expanded.[20]

A short time before the commission filed its report, Martin Luther King marched on Washington, and civil rights emerged as serious congressional business. Although the Commission on the Status of Women declined to equate sexual discrimination with racial discrimination, vindictive opponents of civil rights legislation proposed the addition of a prohibition on sex discrimination to legislation dealing with race, color, religion, or national origin. Liberal and labor-

19. Harrison, "Prelude to Feminism," pp. 130–31
20. U.S. President's Commission on the Status of Women, *American Women: Report of the President's Commission on the Status of Women* (GPO, 1963), p. 45.

oriented congressmen found it prudent to fight the addition but lost, in a 133–168 vote, to a coalition of southerners—whose goal was to complicate life for the civil rights forces—and women members of both parties whose allegiance was to an ERA rather than to protective legislation.

Because protective legislation is inherently discriminatory, inclusion of sex in the Civil Rights Act of 1964 ultimately undercut protective legislation for women. When, in turn, there was no protective legislation that needed protection against an ERA, labor came around in favor of an equal rights amendment. But more than forty years of opposition cannot be made inoperative overnight. Even after formal AFL-CIO endorsement of the ERA in 1973, some labor intellectuals, who all their lives had worshipped Brandeis, the New Deal, Eleanor Roosevelt, and Frances Perkins, found it too hard ever to make the switch.

Escape from Committee

Congressional opponents of civil rights legislation thought it shrewd in 1964 to confound some of their liberal colleagues in the House of Representatives with the proposed addition of sex to the list of proscribed reasons for employment discrimination. The liberals were indeed confounded. Only 40 percent of the members of the House voted to sustain the addition, but it carried because another 40 percent absented themselves from the teller count. Then, civil rights opponents who had plotted intercameral bargaining and who anticipated several opportunities for filibustering unexpectedly found themselves foreclosed from further substantive tampering or procedural maneuvering. To obviate the need for a conference committee, President Johnson had demanded and eventually accomplished Senate approval of the House bill with only minor modifications. The tactical effort to complicate action on civil rights by adding sex discrimination never achieved its purpose; the important sex discrimination language in title VII of the bill backed into law. The Senate never voted on it, and some substantial fraction of the 168 House members who had voted in favor either had no interest in it or probably would have opposed it under other circumstances. The outcome represented, in Gary Orfield's characterization, "an acciden-tal breakthrough."[21]

But legislative accidents show up in the statute books indistinguish-able from deliberate legislative action. With the prohibition written into law, sex discrimination complaints had a legitimate call on the agenda of the Equal Employment Opportunity Commission (EEOC). The complaints turned out to be surprisingly numerous. A Brookings Institution report prepared for the Civil Rights Commission found that the interested groups took very seriously the ban on sex discrimi-nation in title VII and actively pressed cases before the commission.[22] If the sponsors of the sex discrimination amendment wanted to dilute the resources and energy focused on race discrimination, they failed at the congressional and succeeded at the administrative level. Well over one-third of the complaints received in the EEOC's first year alleged sex discrimination.

Equally important, proponents promptly began a campaign to expand the scope of the prohibition by making it applicable to educational institutions and to state and local governments. Women educators and their friends crafted a compelling case against the vulnerable education industry. While expansion of the prohibition against sex discrimination was not accomplished by legislation until 1972, publicity and organizational activity on its behalf comple-mented EEOC investigation and conciliation activity in directing attention to discrimination against women.

In the summer of 1970, Congresswomen Edith Green and Martha Griffiths together outflanked the chairman of the House Judiciary Committee and freed an ERA resolution from twenty-two years of committee captivity without a hearing. From one direction, Green's hearings on legislation to expand prohibitions against sex discrimina-tion in education became de facto hearings on discrimination against women generally and, by implication, hearings on the case for equal rights. With those education subcommittee hearings scheduled to open on June 17, 1970, and to continue for a total of six days during the following two weeks, Griffiths on June 11 moved from another

21. *Congressional Power: Congress and Social Change* (Harcourt Brace Jovanovich, 1975), p. 299. Former Representative Charles Whelan, Jr. (Republican, Ohio) detailed the House action in "Unlikely Hero," *Washington Post,* January 2, 1984.

22. Richard P. Nathan, *Jobs and Civil Rights,* Clearinghouse Publication 16 (GPO, 1969), pp. 50–54.

direction with a petition to discharge the Judiciary Committee from further responsibility for the ERA resolution.

The odds were against success. In 1970 it was a formidable task to take on the chairman of a major standing committee of the House of Representatives. The chances of winning were slim; the likelihood of retribution was great. Sam Rayburn's dictum—"To get along, go along"—still controlled. A few institutional changes had been achieved in 1961 and in 1965 out of concern that an unsympathetic House Rules Committee might frustrate President Kennedy's and then President Johnson's liberal legislative program. In the main, however, the House shied away from proposals to limit the power of committee chairmen, no matter how wide the gap between them and the majority of House Democrats. By the end of the decade, James Sundquist has written, liberal Democrats "were not ready yet to challenge the credentials of Democratic committee chairmen who merely opposed the party's program as distinct from its presidential candidates."[23] So calling a committee meeting, scheduling a hearing, and reporting a bill to the floor remained the exclusive prerogative of the chairman, and becoming chairman remained an exclusive function of seniority.

The power inherent in the position of chairman made it politically dangerous as well as procedurally difficult for a member to challenge a chairman's discretion in connection with meetings, hearings, and reports. Challengers, after all, risked a great deal. Even in the unlikely event of success on a particular bill, in the long run the challenger could not expect to move much else past an embarrassed and probably outraged chairman. In the more likely event of failure, the challenger would have lost his immediate objective, exposed his weakness, and alienated the chairman all at once.

In 1973 and 1975, reformers ended both the system of automatic succession by seniority and the exercise of total authority by a chairman. The relative democratization of the House accomplished by those moves and others during the same years means that House members who challenge a chairman of an important committee are not foreclosing their chances of moving other legislation through the committee. It also means that an unfriendly chairman is not in a position to stifle a hearing, or to decline to report a measure ardently favored by a substantial bloc of members.

23. *The Decline and Resurgence of Congress* (Brookings Institution, 1981), p. 377.

In 1970, that democratization had not yet come to the House. Nevertheless, chairman Emanuel Celler of the House Judiciary Committee was challenged on the ERA by a determined woman member. Faced with the chairman's steadfast unwillingness to call a hearing on the ERA, she persuaded 218 members to sign a discharge petition to by-pass the Judiciary Committee and bring the resolution to the House floor. To that time, in the sixty-year history of the discharge rule, 829 petitions had been filed but only 24 bills were actually discharged. Twenty of them passed the House. Only 2 were enacted into law. Martha Griffiths's ERA discharge petition had a double burden to overcome—first, the traditional and understandable reluctance of members to challenge any important committee chairman, and second, this chairman's strong civil rights record which made it seem illogical to take extraordinary measures against him on a civil rights question. That 218 members would do so bordered on the unthinkable.

Emanuel Celler had represented his Brooklyn district since the Harding administration. His constituency had become partly black but still was composed primarily of middle-class Jews who had moved to Flatbush from the lower east side of Manhattan. Many of the latter worked or had worked in the garment industry where unions remained intensely opposed to an ERA because of its impact on the protective legislation they had struggled to accomplish. Loyalty to the memory of the Brandeis brief and the New Deal was an article of faith. Although Celler rarely set foot in the district, his role in liberalizing immigration law appealed to the Jews, and his work in shepherding various civil rights bills of the late 1950s and 1960s through his committee appealed to the blacks. Since Celler's only jeopardy seemed to lie in his octogenarianism, colleagues who tangled with him would do so at their own risk—at least in the short run.

What moved 218 members of the House to get on a discharge petition that could outrage so powerful and apparently impregnable a chairman—especially when history suggested the petition route probably to be an exercise in futility? Four intertwined explanations suggest themselves.

Fairness. The ERA proposal had been introduced in Congress for forty-seven consecutive years. For twenty-six years, both parties had endorsed it in their quadrennial conventions—the Republicans for thirty years. Yet the Judiciary Committee had not held a hearing on an equal rights amendment for twenty-two years. Celler's attack on "a blunderbuss amendment" which would destroy protective legislation for women reflected statements opposing the amendment by the International Ladies Garment Workers' Evelyn Dubrow, the Amalgamated Clothing Workers' Jacob Potofsky, and the National Urban League's Cernoria Johnson. Celler was entitled to vote his district. He was not entitled to foreclose all formal consideration of a proposal to which both parties had been committed for decades. A member could feel that to sign the petition was not to assure passage of an ERA, but only to endorse a minimum of procedural fairness.

Self-protection. Through the latter part of the 1960s, new organizations of women activists gave promise of becoming important political forces, and old organizations of women gave promise of becoming more politically active. Both the older organizations and the new ones strongly supported an ERA. It was one thing for a congressman facing reelection to deplore the impotence of the individual member in the face of Celler's intransigence, another thing to explain a failure to sign the discharge petition that empowered members to circumvent that intransigence. Electoral self-interest pointed in favor of signing the petition.

Contemporaneous hearings on discrimination. Edith Green's hearings on discrimination against women gave members a logical and reasonable rationalization for signing. No one doubts that important legislation, and most of all a constitutional amendment, should come to the floor with a hearings record that establishes the case for the legislation, examines its probable consequences, and perfects its language. Absent such a record, the House is likely to be accused of acting capriciously. In the case of the ERA, members seemed compelled to choose between dangers—on the one hand, the danger of acting without a record of preliminary work; on the other hand, the danger of not acting because preliminary work was foreclosed. The petition was filed exactly because there had been no House hearings on ERA in over two decades. But without a hearings record to point to, how could support be rationalized?

Part of the necessary rationalization could have been found in the Senate Judiciary subcommittee's hearings on the ERA in May 1970.[24] Those hearings had been provoked by aggressive action of the Na-

---

24. *The "Equal Rights" Amendment,* Hearings before the Subcommittee on Constitutional Amendments of the Senate Judiciary Committee, 91 Cong. 2 sess. (GPO, 1970).

tional Organization for Women during subcommittee consideration earlier that year of the amendment giving eighteen-year-olds the right to vote. The NOW demonstrators demanded hearings on the ERA. "As a direct result of that confrontation on that occasion," Senator Marlow W. Cook, Republican of Kentucky, later recalled, "hearings were scheduled on this proposed [equal rights] amendment."[25] Interested groups, analysts, and constitutional lawyers had filled the record at the Senate hearings. Neither chamber, however, is often disposed to recognize let alone acknowledge the sufficiency of the other chamber's hearings. In this case, House opponents of an ERA who had barred a House hearing now could be expected to deplore its absence.

Hearings on discrimination against women before Green's House education subcommittee served as surrogate for Judiciary Committee hearings on an equal rights amendment—hearings that never were. "I hope," said Green, "that the various kinds of discrimination against women in our society will be discussed and will be fully documented, and that this can be made available to the men who run the world."[26] Over seven days of hearings, women witnesses documented inequality and discrimination not only in education, but also in the civil service; in the professions, including law and medicine; in employment; and in vocational counseling. Whether or not the data entered in the record at Green's hearings became "available to the men who run the world," her hearings served the ERA cause brilliantly.

Green's own independent record gave wavering members confidence in the hearings. By 1970, Edith Green of Oregon, whose congressional career began in 1954, had become a maverick. She was second-ranking Democrat on the House Education and Labor Committee where she had started as a flaming liberal when conservative Democrats ran the committee. As liberals took command in the 1960s, Green moved to the right, especially on issues of state and local control. While Green often spoke out against "the discrimination against women which still permeates our society," she was more unpredictable than predictable. For example, she broke sharply with other women in the House when she alone among them sided against

25. *Equal Rights 1970*, Hearings before the Senate Judiciary Committee, 91 Cong. 2 sess. (GPO, 1970), pp. 293, 297.

26. *Discrimination Against Women*, Hearings before the Special Subcommittee on Education of the House Education and Labor Committee, 91 Cong. 2 sess. (GPO, 1970), pt. 1, p. 4.

inclusion of sex discrimination in the 1964 civil rights legislation. Because Green was not thought to be riding a hobby horse, her 1970 hearings on discrimination against women—the right hearings at the right time—played a critical role in greasing the way for the ERA to achieve a first-ever vote on the floor of the House.

Martha Griffiths's determination. Griffiths could not match Celler's influence over legislation as a committee chairman. She was, however, not powerless. A member of the Ways and Means Committee which then still controlled the committee assignments of House Democrats, Griffiths both held and could offer IOUs. She could also be helpful or difficult with special problems involving trade and tax measures. For some members, joining Griffiths's side seemed an investment in the future—she was fifty-eight, Celler was eighty-two. Griffiths worked the House shamelessly. "I didn't let anyone forget this one," she has said of the petition drive. "I chased fellow congressmen ruthlessly."[27] One example is then Democratic whip Hale Boggs of Louisiana, who was not sympathetic to the proposed amendment but agreed to sign the petition if 199 others did so before him. They did, and he did. The eventual 218 signatures included 155 Democrats and 63 Republicans.

When, six weeks after the petition was filed, Griffiths triumphantly announced that she had 218 signatures, Emanuel Celler tried to regain control of a situation that threatened soon to be entirely beyond his control. Celler scheduled Judiciary Committee hearings on the ERA for September 16—"the first available date." Griffiths declined the bait. She decided instead to push her apparent advantage despite the real possibility that some members, including some who had signed her petition, would back off and take cover behind Celler's offer of orderly procedure. A few days before calling up the petition, Griffiths reminded potential delinquents of her intention to act the following week. "I hope you all are here," she remarked pointedly to House colleagues, many of whom might have preferred to be absent.[28] Before the vote, Griffiths dismissed the pro forma objections of ranking members of the Judiciary Committee that an amendment to the Constitution should not be subject to "hasty, ill-considered action."

27. Hope Chamberlin, *A Minority of Members: Women in the U.S. Congress* (Praeger, 1973), p. 259.
28. *Congressional Record,* vol. 116 (1970), p. 27447.

Since the proposal had been offered for forty-seven consecutive years and the committee had resisted hearings on it for more than two decades, her resort to an extraordinary procedure hardly translated into hasty action. Nor was there an available remedy for women aside from constitutional change, according to Griffiths, because "there never was a time when decisions of the Supreme Court could not have done everything we ask today. . . [but] the Court has held for 98 years that women, as a class, are not entitled to equal protection of the laws." The Court was not running for reelection, but most members of the House were. They voted overwhelmingly (332–22) in favor of the discharge resolution and even more overwhelmingly (352–15) in favor of the ERA.[29]

On the Senate side, ironically, hearings in a generally sympathetic Judiciary subcommittee followed by additional hearings in the full committee seemed to produce more trouble for the ERA than did Celler's efforts to suppress the resolution without a hearing in his House committee. Organized labor's massive reversal of position had not yet come about, so senators confronted a record of firm opposition to the resolution by, among others, the Clothing Workers, the Ladies Garment Workers, the Hotel and Restaurant Employees, and the AFL-CIO's own legislative spokesman. All of them viewed with alarm the possibility that an equal rights amendment would invalidate protective labor laws and standards.

Members of the House who had supported the amendment over labor's objections could at least plead an empty record on the protective legislation issue. Since senators could not, they found another way out of the dilemma. The ERA came to the Senate floor in October 1970, when as many as thirty members were out campaigning, and at best only a few weeks remained in the life of the Ninety-first Congress. It was no secret that Celler would stall action on the House side if a conference committee were made necessary by a Senate amendment to the House-passed resolution. Consequently, when the Senate adopted (36–33) an amendment that allowed Congress to exempt women from the draft, chances ended for congressional passage of the ERA in 1970.

Not all supporters of the resolution regretted the outcome. Adoption of the draft-exemption proviso had more to do with how to go

29. Ibid., pp. 28005, 28004, 28036–37.

about amending the Constitution than it did with women's equality. Had the Senate adopted the House version of the resolution, Congress would have proposed a constitutional amendment after only one hour of debate in the House where, for whatever reasons, there had been no hearings, and after end-of-session consideration by the Senate when nearly one-third of its members were absent. While some congressmen are simply posturing when they deplore efforts to amend the Constitution without long and intense consideration, most legislators do attach a special importance to change in the written Constitution. The Senate was the end of the line. Without a fuller legislative history, a majority of senators facing a vote on the ERA in 1970 could not bring themselves to send on to the states the amendment passed by the House.

By adopting an amendment to the House language, senators showed concern about the paucity of congressional debate on the ERA without voting against it. Given its strength in the House, the ERA could be expected to pass again in the next Congress under more deliberative—that is, leisurely—circumstances. The ERA's most ardent Senate sponsor, Democrat Birch Bayh of Indiana, imparted no sense of emergency. "The most important reason for enacting this amendment is its symbolic value," Bayh was saying at the time.[30] If symbolism was the dominant consideration, it cut two ways in that it was also important to preserve the symbol of the Constitution as a document not easily tampered with.

Once Griffiths managed the discharge resolution to a House vote, the ERA became a realistic objective that women's groups could not put aside. Until then, fundamental change in the way the House ruled itself seemed to be a prerequisite for consideration of the ERA. Reform of the House rules and practices to weaken the control of committee chairmen impressed some women as more complex a preliminary step than they thought it practical to contemplate— especially since no one could be sure that an ERA resolution, if it could come to the floor, would survive the opposition of most of organized labor. But in the instant case, the procedural barrier cracked under pressure from Griffiths. Almost at the same time, labor's united dedication to saving protective legislation also cracked as the United Auto Workers, Griffiths' constituents, put themselves on record

30. Ibid., p. 35452.

against protective legislation affecting women only, and in favor of the ERA.

No longer just a far-out vision of a small group, beginning in 1970 the ERA became an implicit test of the political strength of the women's movement. For the next two decades at least, the movement would be both nourished and drained by the ERA cause. It became the most-wanted objective of the modern women's movement. Loyalty, prestige, and resources were all involved. From time to time there really was light at the end of the tunnel. With a few better breaks, this war might have been won quickly and with relatively little bloodshed.

Success in Congress

Martha Griffiths started again in 1971, this time from a position of strength. Celler, who in earlier years had been simultaneously unwilling to permit the ERA to come to a hearing in his committee and insistent that the resolution not be reported without a hearing, quickly assigned the proposal to Judiciary's Civil and Constitutional Rights Subcommittee, chaired by Don Edwards, a liberal California Democrat. If the decision to ignore labor opposition had worried some members in 1970, the intervening election provided reassurance that support for an ERA would not put a congressman on labor's list of enemies. The AFL-CIO's chief lobbyist still spoke of the "potentially destructive impact" of the ERA on women's protective legislation,[31] but everyone knew that organized labor was of two minds and might very well change sides itself.

Edwards brought the ERA through his subcommittee with a recommendation for adoption without amendment. While Celler managed to have the full Judiciary Committee add amendments allowing Congress to continue exempting women from the draft and permitting Congress or the states to enact protective labor standards for women, it was his last hurrah. Like the discharge petition in 1970, the House vote in 1971 to drop the committee's amendments exposed Celler's weakened position and highlighted the strength of the ERA

---

31. Andrew J. Biemiller, in *Equal Rights for Men and Women, 1971,* Hearings, p. 332.

proposal. Once again, the resolution passed by an overwhelming majority. (A year later, Celler would lose the Democratic primary for the seat he had held since 1923. Celler's congressional service that began the year Charles Curtis had first introduced an ERA thus ended the year Congress finally passed an ERA. In the ultimate ironical touch, his nemesis in the primary was a woman with a passion for the ERA.)

When the equal rights amendment passed the Senate on March 22, 1972, it appeared to be riding an irresistible high. The Judiciary Committee had reported the resolution without amendment on a 15–1 vote. Hugh Scott of Pennsylvania, Republican leader in the Senate, then solicited and got an endorsement from President Nixon. "Throughout 21 years," the president wrote, "I have not altered my belief that equal rights for women warrant a constitutional guarantee—and I therefore continue to favor the enactment of the constitutional amendment to achieve this goal."[32] During two days of floor debate, the "pure" language favored by sponsors was never in jeopardy. Only one of nine amendments proposed by Senator Sam J. Ervin, Jr., Democrat of North Carolina, to preserve special protection or treatment for women attracted as many as 18 votes, and that one—to safeguard laws that exempt women from service in combat units—lost 71–18. Final passage came 84–8, a luxurious 22 votes more than the required two-thirds.[33]

Ervin's objections to an equal rights amendment, detailed in twenty-six pages of minority report, merit attention as probably the most comprehensive and careful statement of opposition made by a public official. While two of his six points are rhetorical flourishes—that a majority of both sexes did not want an amendment, and that an ERA would have a "radical effect" on American social structure—four points in his minority report present substantive questions. Ervin argued that the Fourteenth Amendment already provided women all the protection they could secure from an ERA; that state and federal laws and federal executive orders, as well as then-recent legal developments, gave ample specific protection; that an equal rights amendment would have undesirable effects on the military, on

32. "Letter to the Senate Minority Leader about the Proposed Constitutional Amendment on Equal Rights for Men and Women, March 18, 1972," *Public Papers of the Presidents: Richard Nixon, 1972* (GPO, 1974), p. 444.
33. *Congressional Record,* vol. 118 (1972), p. 9598.

criminal and domestic relations law, and on protective labor legislation; that an ERA would violate the right to privacy in schools, restrooms, dormitories, and prisons.[34] After the Senate rejected all of these contentions, and adopted the House-passed resolution, no claim could be made that Congress acted in ignorance of the asserted consequences—legal and constitutional—of an ERA.

A high level of optimism seemed well warranted. The ERA proposal could not be attacked as excessively novel or as one that politicians and the public needed time to understand—it had after all first been offered forty-nine years earlier. It was free of the warning signal that automatically attaches to bills and resolutions that squeak through one or both houses of Congress by a close vote—House passage had been by nearly fifteen to one and Senate passage by better than ten to one. Congressional action reflected a bipartisan effort— not only had strong backing for the Democratic-sponsored ERA come from leaders of both parties and from the Republican president, even the handful of opposition votes divided between Democrats and Republicans. Unless experienced and politically sensitive federal officeholders were wildly out of touch with sentiment in the states, or compelling new considerations were to surface, or proponents were to commit some egregious blunder, ratification then seemed a foregone conclusion.

Whatever it was, something went wrong.

Born Again, Dead Again

Various kinds of troubles not present in 1972 faced the ERA when sponsors announced its political resurrection in 1982. One of them was trouble with Republicans in high places. Both the Republican president of the United States and the Republican chairman of the Senate Judiciary Committee vigorously opposed the amendment. Ten years earlier, a different Republican president had favored the ERA, and so did his Republican successor. In 1972, the Judiciary chairman was a Democrat, but the then-ranking Republican member favored the amendment. The Republican national platform for 1972 endorsed the ERA, and so did the platform in 1976. But the 1980

34. *Equal Rights for Men and Women,* S.Rept.92–689, 92 Cong. 2 sess. (GPO, 1972).

platform only "reaffirmed" a commitment to equal rights, and it pointedly omitted an endorsement of the ERA.[35]

There was new trouble, too, with serious students of the Constitution. Some of them were disaffected by the congressional action in 1979 extending by simple majority vote of each house the ratification deadline specified in the joint resolution passed in 1972 by two-thirds votes. Others who adhered to "contemporaneous consensus" as a desirable principle underlying constitutional change, doubted whether a proposal that could not achieve consensus in ten years should be renewed promptly. Still others concluded that whatever its merits the ERA would now create an undesirable constitutional "clutter" because its major purposes had been achieved over the preceding decade by legislative and judicial action. One old trouble surfaced again as some constitutional scholars found the imprecise language of the ERA an invitation to prolonged adjudication.[36]

If Republican leaders and constitutional purists were not enough, trouble over strategy obtained within the ranks of the supposedly devout. Some activist women favored at least a pause as a matter of strategy in order to let emotions cool. Others thought a prolonged pause in the ERA drive worthwhile in order to organize on behalf of different legislative goals that had taken second place to the amendment. And still others thought a pause obligatory so that the condition of the women's movement—especially the impact of the abortion dispute on it—could be assessed and plans could be laid for further strengthening it.

For all the important opponents and the doubters, however, the ERA continued to enjoy support in high places even after its near-enshrinement in the Constitution had instead become a rejection card that read "Return to GO." "That we have so much support in the House and Senate should amaze those who claimed the ERA effort would die on June 30, [1982]," said Representative Patricia Schroeder, the Colorado Democrat who became the proposal's leading

35. "We acknowledge the legitimate efforts of those who support or oppose ratification of the Equal Rights Amendment. We reaffirm our Party's historic commitment to equal rights and equality for women." Republican Platform 1980, *Congressional Quarterly Almanac, 1980,* p. 613.

36. See, for example, Lincoln Oliphant, "Toward a New ERA?" *National Review* (June 24, 1983), pp. 742–45.

congressional sponsor. "Like the phoenix rising from the ashes," she added, "the effort is stronger than ever."[37]

But this phoenix was twice-consumed—once in the ratification failure, and again in subsequent rejection by the House. For the ERA's proponents and for its opponents, the question is whether the fault lay in their stars or in themselves. The answer is of more than academic interest because it should define the strategy and timing of a renewed effort—and predict its prospects.

37. *Congressional Record,* daily edition (July 14, 1982), p. H4063.

Chapter Two

Postmortems

IN THE SPRING OF 1972 the addition of an equal rights amendment to the Constitution seemed assured. The Ninety-second Congress displayed a near-unanimity on the subject that House and Senate more commonly show for approval of the previous day's journal than for approval of a constitutional amendment dealing with social relations and social change. Were it not for the loyalty shown by most Judiciary Committee members to their chairman, the opposition vote in the House of Representatives—insignificant as it was at twenty-four— would have been reduced to a trace. On the Senate side, Sam Ervin's prolonged fight against the proposal brought a total of only eight nays on the final roll call. Both houses overwhelmingly rejected language, comparable to that adopted in the Senate in earlier years, that would have limited the sweep of the ERA. What for decades had been impossible to accomplish was now accomplished.

The triumph of the ERA in Congress was complete, deliberate, and overpowering, an outcome clearly attributable to a congressional perception that a national consensus had been achieved. In the quarter century between the end of World War II and passage of the ERA, Congress avoided sending on to the states any controversial proposals for constitutional change; none passed except proposals that commanded complete and overpowering support. In turn, during that period the states routinely ratified all five amendments to the Constitution proposed to them. Three deal with choosing a president—the two-term limit, presidential disability and succession, and voting rights in presidential elections for residents of the District of Columbia. The remaining two also deal with voting rights—prohibition of a poll tax requirement, and extending the vote to eighteen-year-olds. By the time Congress acted on the latter two, neither was still controversial. The two-term limit and presidential disability amendments address governmental structure rather than substantive rights; and the limited franchise granted the District's population

26

provides it only a tiny fraction of the electoral college total—3 votes of 538.

The ERA is not a structural question, nor would it be of only marginal consequence. But the Congress that finally passed the ERA believed itself to be taking on no more divisive a question than its predecessors took on in passing the previous five proposals. Congress did not decide to avoid the hard question of equal rights for women by passing it on to the states. Rather, Congress vetted the question and deemed it sufficiently settled to merit constitutional status. If Congress had had final rather than penultimate responsibility for constitutional change, the vote probably would have been unchanged. When the ratification process began, all the signs—overwhelming approval by Congress in an era when an apparently discriminating Congress only approved winners, unqualified backing from a strong and still-popular president, repeated endorsements by both political parties in their national platforms—presaged easy and quick success. The ERA instead died a slow death, its downhill slide virtually unchecked for the last eight years of its ten-year fight for life.

Through all those years, polling data reported support for the ERA from a majority of the adult population to have held firm. In October 1974, the Gallup public opinion referendum ballot that forces a "favor" or "oppose" choice on respondents produced a 78 percent favorable vote, with 22 percent opposed.[1] At least a two-thirds majority from each major group supported "a constitutional amendment which would give women equal rights and equal responsibilities." In each of the eight subsequent years except 1977 and 1979, Gallup asked respondents who had heard of the proposal "Do you favor or oppose this amendment?" and also offered a "no opinion" option. Among those who had heard of the ERA, the percentage of favorable answers never fell below 56, that of opposition responses never exceeded 34. Although support was marginally weaker in the Midwest and South, even those regions consistently showed comfortable majorities for the ERA. Intermittent reports on national polls from other major polling organizations indicated equally favorable results. Accurately enough, three political scientists who reviewed the

1. *Gallup Opinion Index*, no. 113 (November 1974), p. 17; no. 118 (April 1975), pp. 20–21; no. 128 (March 1976), pp. 18–19; no. 178 (June 1980), p. 4; no. 190 (July 1981), pp. 24–25; no. 203 (August 1982), p. 28.

polling data after the loss of the amendment titled their report, "The ERA Won—At Least in the Opinion Polls."[2] That the ERA failed, however, in the polls that really counted—those conducted in fifteen state legislatures—cannot be gainsaid.

What went wrong? "We underestimated" is a common beginning to explanations offered by proponents. But considerable difference of opinion obtains about what in particular was underestimated and about the importance of one or another putative underestimate as a determinant of the outcome. For example, some proponents believe the huge congressional majorities and favorable national opinion polls lulled them into underestimating how effectively the Constitution stacks the deck against substantive amendment, and that their failure to address that phenomenon early enough doomed the ERA. The proposition merits closer attention. So do those postmortems that variously attribute the outcome to underestimates of the indifference of different presidents, the success of in lieu approaches, the survival needs of women's organizations, or some women's anxieties about how an equal rights amendment would affect them.

The Amendment Process as Stacked Deck

Madison's defense of the mode preferred by the constitutional convention for achieving alteration calls it one that "seems to be stamped with every mark of propriety. It guards equally against that extreme facility, which would render the Constitution too mutable; and that extreme difficulty, which might perpetuate its discovered faults."[3] After two hundred years of experience, a modern assessment by Professor Paul Brest reaches a less soothing judgment: "The procedures in Article V for constitutional amendment are designedly obstacle-ridden and antimajoritarian."[4]

The deck is more and more stacked against change, the argument goes, because a pluralist system spawns increasingly contentious and specialized groups. Consequently, substantive change in the Constitution is virtually debarred by the proliferation of narrow interests that

2. Mark R. Daniels, Robert Darcy, and Joseph W. Westphal, "The ERA Won—At Least in the Opinion Polls," *PS* (Fall 1982), pp. 578–84.

3. James Madison, *The Federalist,* no. 43.

4. *Processes of Constitutional Decisionmaking* (Little, Brown, 1975), p. 978.

cannot be fused. The ERA, like any proposal for substantive change, does well to command a comfortable majority but simply cannot hope to achieve the extraordinary majorities required first in Congress and then among the states.

Even accepting the case for extraordinary majorities in dealing with change in the fundamental law leaves open the question of how much of an extraordinary majority is reasonable to demand. Two-thirds? Three-fifths? Three-fourths? Consider that the Senate in 1975 found unreasonable the extraordinary majority its own rules had long imposed for terminating a filibuster. Members amended those rules to permit closure by three-fifths of all senators rather than two-thirds of those voting. Not all senators agree in their assessments of the change, but Walter F. Mondale, Minnesota Democrat, who served before and after the new rule, has argued that it changed the entire atmosphere, discouraged and shortened filibusters, and resulted in closure being invoked earlier and more frequently.[5] No voice is heard protesting that the change has stifled important minorities.

Three-fourths of the whole is the most substantial majority imposed anywhere in the American political system. The founders were content even to dissolve the Articles of Confederation and establish the Constitution itself upon ratification by only nine of thirteen, or seven-tenths, of the states: "The ratification of the conventions of nine states shall be sufficient for the establishment of this Constitution between the States so ratifying the same."[6] While the original Constitution would not have been binding on nonratifying states, and an amendment binds all the states, escalation from seven-tenths to a three-fourths ratification requirement means that the founders chose to make it harder to effect constitutional change than to create the union.

The ERA, then, may be facing a stacked deck, a problem comparable to that faced by other proposals for substantive change in the Constitution. In two hundred years, about ten thousand constitutional amendments have been offered. Of the twenty-six amendments adopted, ten for all practical purposes came as a package with the original document, while only some bending of the rules allowed the

---

5. Cited in James L. Sundquist, *The Decline and Resurgence of Congress* (Brookings Institution, 1981), p. 395.
6. *Constitution of the United States,* Article VII.

Thirteenth, Fourteenth, and Fifteenth Amendments to be ratified.[7] The roster of recent efforts that failed in Congress includes proposed amendments dealing with school busing, school prayer, abortion, and a balanced federal budget.

Still, the hypothesis of a stacked deck is not a satisfactory explanation of the loss of the ERA if only because the proposed amendment came so far. Once Congress proposes an amendment, ratification is the norm, rejection the exception. While virtually all proposed amendments lose, virtually all are unable to attract the necessary two-thirds of both houses of Congress in the first place. Most proposals for constitutional amendment are deemed by congressional leaders to be without merit, unworthy of even a hearing. Others may eventually command a bare congressional majority, yet lack support from even three-fifths—the minimum extraordinary majority known to the system. Still others that command widespread support are accomplished without formal change in the Constitution. Proposed amendments that actually pass Congress only to founder in the states constitute an especially select group of seven—just three since the Civil War. Child labor ultimately was mooted by adoption of the Fair Labor Standards Act and the decision of the Supreme Court upholding the act's constitutionality. The ERA expired after ten and a quarter years. Congressional representation for the District of Columbia, given only seven years from August 1978 to achieve ratification, directly affects fewer than a million people, concentrated in one area, but significantly dilutes the voting power in the Senate of each of the fifty states. The proposed amendment to achieve it could barely muster the needed two-thirds majorities in House and Senate. That it could do so at all is as much a denial of the stacked deck generalization as its inability to be ratified may seem to be a confirmation.

The Constitution is hard to amend; it is by no means impossible to amend. In this century, six amendments were adopted between 1913 and 1933, five between 1951 and 1971. Successful efforts at constitutional change have addressed both procedural and substantive matters. Prohibition and its repeal, the income tax, and woman

---

7. Andrew C. McLaughlin notes that on the three post–Civil War amendments, the states that had seceded "were, it seems, sufficiently alive to sanction formally a constitutional amendment, but not, as yet, far enough revived to be received into full participation in legislative halls." *A Constitutional History of the United States* (Appleton-Century, 1935), pp. 635–36.

suffrage—all of them controversial questions—worked their way through the amendment process. In the last analysis, the ERA turns out to be the principal example of the supposed stacked deck—which makes stacked deck more a rationalization for its loss than an explanation of its loss.

Different and Indifferent Presidents

Supporters of the ERA especially deplore President Reagan's outright opposition to it.[8] No president, however, wins their unqualified praise as a hero of the cause. "We have had Johnson's daughter and Carter's daughter-in-law and Ford's wife," one ERA stalwart says, "but only Nixon made himself useful and we probably didn't really need him at the time." Is loss of the ERA attributable to the various degrees of indifference exhibited by different presidents even before President Reagan showed outright hostility?

Presidents who professed to be friendly were not friendly enough to take a leadership role—a reluctance that ERA people find especially troublesome. Some of the latter who focus on presidential indifference as an important determinant of the outcome argue that the amendment might well have been enacted in the 1950s if an oddly phrased apparent endorsement of the ERA in Eisenhower's January 1957 budget message ("The platforms of both major parties have advocated an amendment of the Constitution to insure equal rights for women. I believe that Congress should make certain that women are not denied equal rights with men.")[9] had been the forerunner of presidential involvement. It was not, however, and Cynthia E. Harrison's study of the women's movement in that period judges the administration's position to be ambiguous, rather than unequivocal:

The Eisenhower White House did support the Amendment, although

8. *Washington Post,* November 29, 1983, quoted Judy Goldsmith, president of the National Organization for Women: "There's little question in my mind that it's more important to defeat Ronald Reagan [than to pass the ERA]. . . . If we had to choose one of the two, I would choose the defeat of Ronald Reagan. The ERA can wait one more year." Reagan's position on the ERA is set forth most extensively in an interview with Ann Devron in *Weekly Compilation of Presidential Documents* (August 29, 1983), pp. 1166–67.

9. *Public Papers of the Presidents: Dwight D. Eisenhower, 1957* (Government Printing Office, 1958), p. 57.

too weakly to be decisive in the legislative fight. In fact, the President's staff did not even insist that the Department of Labor follow its suit. Therefore, in an attempt to mollify organized labor, the Department maintained its opposition although it was tempered in comparison with the previous Democratic administrations. The Women's Bureau, on the other hand, withdrew its opposition to the ERA. It did not, however, actively champion either the Amendment or any alternative plan to upgrade women's status. The Women's Bureau coalition thus found itself without its customary leader. Congressional adherents to the Bureau's former position held the line on the ERA and throughout the 1950s the stalemate continued, with no progress made to secure women's rights.[10]

Subsequent presidents and presidential nominees until 1980 allowed their national party platform to repeat the ritualistic endorsement of an ERA. President Johnson might have persuaded Emanuel Celler to unlock the Judiciary Committee closet to which Celler consigned the ERA, but Johnson's interests and priorities, like those of John F. Kennedy, were with other causes. The report of the President's Commission on the Status of Women, a commission appointed by Kennedy, did not call for passage of an ERA.[11] Nor did either Kennedy or Johnson. It fell to President Nixon's Task Force on Women's Rights and Responsibilities to become the first such group to declare for an ERA.[12] Since it is understood that a presidential task force report rarely reaches conclusions uninfluenced by the preferences of its principal sponsor, the presumption of presidential support made it easier for Republicans to sign Martha Griffiths's discharge petition in the House. Further, Nixon's endorsement of the amendment, sent to Republican leader Hugh Scott of Pennsylvania just before the final Senate vote, does qualify as useful follow-through.

The hard cases to evaluate in a review of presidential efforts on behalf of the ERA are those of Presidents Ford and Carter, both nominal supporters, and both without much to show in the way of results. As Republican leader of the House, Ford had an ambiguous position on the ERA. Fifteen of the last sixteen signatures on Martha Griffiths's discharge petition in 1970 were furnished by Republicans.

10. "Prelude to Feminism: Women's Organizations, the Federal Government and the Rise of the Women's Movement, 1942 to 1968" (Ph.D. dissertation, Columbia University, 1982), p. 101.

11. U.S. President's Commission on the Status of Women, *American Women: Report of the President's Commission on the Status of Women* (GPO, 1963).

12. Presidential Task Force on Women's Rights and Responsibilities, *A Matter of Simple Justice* (GPO, 1970), pp. 4–5.

"I had something to do with [that] fact," Ford said after the petition was filed[13]—yet his own signature was not one of them.

When Ford succeeded Nixon in August 1974, the ERA had been ratified by thirty-three states. By August, the high season of state legislative activity for 1974 was past so that, as a practical matter, Ford had only two years in which he might have tried to influence ratification. His approach to adoption of the ERA was to be sympathetic, not personally aggressive. President Ford chose to cheer Betty Ford on from the sidelines rather than to get in the line himself and block. "In the next session of the [Illinois] legislature, would you get on the phone and call some local Republicans, asking, urging them to pass the ERA?" the president was asked in Chicago in July 1975, after the Illinois house had ratified the ERA, leaving its ultimate fate in Illinois to the state senate. "Well," he replied, "I think Betty does a fine job in this effort. I, of course, voted for the Equal Rights Amendment when I was in the Congress. My record is clear. She is an effective spokesman, and I see no decrease in her enthusiasm for this. So, come next year, I suspect she can speak for both of us."[14]

Translated from political language, the message was that Ford would be glad enough to see the ERA ratified but did not plan to spend personal political-capital on the project. Save for a routine proclamation of Women's Equality Day in August 1976 that included a call to states that had not ratified "to give serious consideration" to ratification, for two critical years President Ford left the ERA to his wife even as its momentum slowed and signs of trouble became increasingly apparent.

Like his predecessor, Jimmy Carter pointed to his wife's work on behalf of the ERA, but unlike Ford, Carter contemplated using the office to put pressure on states to ratify. Identifying the textile industry and the John Birch Society as strong and effective opponents of the ERA in the South, Carter said he planned to stand up to them. "As President," Carter said in March 1976, eight months before the election, "I will use the influence of the office" to see that the amendment becomes law. "I intend to see the passage of the Equal Rights Amendment."[15] Given the stated intention of candidate Carter

13. *Congressional Record,* vol. 116 (1970), p. 28016.

14. *The Presidential Campaign, 1976,* vol. 2, pt. 1: *President Gerald R. Ford* (GPO, 1979), p. 8.

15. Ibid., vol. 1, pt. 1: *Jimmy Carter,* pp. 94, 222.

regarding the ERA, it is especially noteworthy that during Carter's incumbency no state ratified the proposal. The last to do so, Indiana, completed action two days before his inauguration.

For all practical purposes, however, little more time was available to Carter as president than had been available to Ford in which to negotiate with state politicians about ratification. By the fall of 1977, ERA proponents had a new idea—to protect their investment by extending the ratification period beyond the seven years specified in the original resolution. When cooperative congressmen moved to transform that idea from pipe dream to legitimate legislative proposal, ratification efforts took a back seat to extension efforts.

The campaign to achieve an extension relieved President Carter of responsibility for a last-ditch effort to press or bargain with holdouts in the state legislatures. Carter's first year in office—or at least most of the first year—was the sole period in his term during which the ratification rules adopted in 1972 were neither about to be revised nor already revised. For that reason as well as because a president is likely to be strongest in his first year, 1977 was the prime time for Carter to act on the ERA. But the problem required strategic planning to protect the new president from charges of disregard for the principles of the federal system. That planning was never done, the "influence of the office" not used on behalf of ratification.

If there is a case for the proposition that presidential indifference after 1972 accounts for the loss of the ERA, most of the case must rest on President Ford's response. Consider that up until Nixon preoccupied himself with Watergate, there had been no reason to make a further special effort for the ERA. By August 1974, when Nixon resigned, thirty-three states had ratified, three of them earlier that year. Majorities were shrinking below two-thirds but were still comfortably wide.[16] At the other end, Carter came to the presidency after the ratification battle had hardened and almost at the point where the substantive question of ratification had been temporarily eclipsed by the procedural question of an extension of time to accomplish it. President Ford managed to espouse support of the ERA but to give it a low priority when it would have benefited most from a high priority.

16. Maine ratified on January 18, 1974, by 78–68 and 19–11 in the house and senate, respectively; Montana on January 21, 1974, by 73–23 and 28–22; Ohio on February 7, 1974, by 54–40 and 20–12.

Yet, Ford was not singularly indifferent to the ERA. His tenure is not marked by dramatic activity in any controversial area. The bad luck of the ERA is that during two crucial years when it most needed a strategist of the Lyndon Johnson or Richard Nixon school, Gerald Ford found it expedient to hand this ball off to his wife.

In Lieu Approaches

By July 1, 1982, as much in the way of equal rights for women may have been achieved by state constitutional changes along with federal statute, executive action, and judicial opinions as would have been achieved with ratification of the proposed amendment. Jo Freeman, a political scientist and an active feminist, wrote in 1975, even when it was still very much alive, that the ERA's most valuable effect would be the psychological victory it would provide women. Whatever acute problems women then faced, Freeman wrote in *The Politics of Women's Liberation,* would not be solved by the ERA. "At best, it will clear up some legal deadwood that might well be eliminated by judicial and legislative decisions without it.... The specific legal consequences of the ERA itself are not really worth the effort that has been put into it."[17]

Even those on the same side of a legislative struggle may have different judgments about whether they won or lost. Some adherents to any public policy cause will decide that an apparent victory is illusory and that the fight must be continued; others will embrace even a partial success and go on to new fights. Many activist women do not view ERA as a goal for which there is no honorable substitute. Like Freeman, they argue that the most compelling need for it preceded the body of favorable legislative actions and judicial rulings that appeared in the 1960s and 1970s. While NOW's Eleanor Smeal said of the ERA as it died, "We have no other agenda," others hold that pursuit of the constitutional amendment should not be allowed to continue to dominate the women's policy agenda.[18]

According to this view, the ERA is only transfigured rather than

17. (Longman, 1975), pp. 238, 240.
18. *Washington Post,* June 27, 1982; also see the comments of a former president of the Women's Lobby and those of the president of the National Abortion Rights Action League in *New York Times,* May 20, 1982.

dead, and those supporters who mistakenly assume that formal amendment is the sole route to constitutional change should be reminded of what Clement Vose calls the "open secret" that Congress and the president also have generated statutes and executive orders that are fundamental law. As Vose explains the varieties of ways of engaging in constitutional warfare and achieving public policy objectives, change in the language of the formal document is only the most obvious: "No legal decree wins compliance simply because of its form, and a policy placed in the United States Constitution does not necessarily carry more weight than the same order adopted as a statute, issued as a presidential executive order or issued as a ruling by the Supreme Court."[19]

Equal pay or equal educational opportunity epitomizes equal rights for some women. On their list of social policy priorities, other aspects of women's rights rank below programs for children, the aged, or the mentally ill. Equal rights stalwarts, while working for passage of one or another discrete legislative approach to equality, worry about the weakening effects of discrete victories that focus on pay or education or insurance. With each such victory, some enthusiasts for the ERA lose interest in the amendment itself. The oldest and most far-reaching goal of the modern women's movement could be shelved indefinitely if more and more participants in the movement see their separate priorities achieved. So be it, say those who welcome such achievement. A diminished enthusiasm for the ERA even among its supporting groups should not be cause for concern, or be interpreted as loss of interest in equal rights. Any group that gains satisfaction from the judges and presidents in power naturally sheds its preoccupation with formal amendment.

The underlying theme of the women's movement—equality to replace inequality wherever it may exist under law—probably precludes satisfaction from judges and congressmen and presidents adequate to induce permanent abandonment of interest in a formal ERA. Satisfaction through action short of consitutional amendment comes more readily to a cause more specific than "equality of rights under the law."

Disposition of the child labor amendment is a case in point. In its 1918 decision in *Hammer* v. *Dagenhart,* the Supreme Court struck

19. *Constitutional Change* (D.C. Heath, 1972), p. 65.

down a statutory prohibition on interstate commerce in the products of child labor.[20] An effort then began to give Congress constitutional power to effect that prohibition. Submitted to the states in 1924 without a time limit for ratification, by 1937 an amendment empowering Congress to "limit, regulate, and prohibit" child labor had been ratified by twenty-eight states, eight short of the necessary number. Not on the presidential agenda of either Calvin Coolidge or Herbert Hoover, the cause fared better with President Roosevelt. Still, his letter sent early in 1937 to each of nineteen governors urging that ratification of the pending amendment be made a major item of the state's business that year did not get the job done.[21] At Roosevelt's request, however, Congress in 1938 enacted a Fair Labor Standards Act that prohibited shipment in interstate commerce of any goods produced by "any oppressive child labor."[22] Three years later, the Supreme Court found the twenty-three-year-old decision in *Hammer* v. *Dagenhart* "a departure from the principles which prevailed in the interpretation of the commerce clause.... It should be and now is overruled."[23] The anti–child labor forces found the transformation of fundamental law complete. Finally satisfied by the president, Congress, and judges in power, opponents of child labor abandoned their preoccupation with a constitutional amendment.

The comparability of the child labor cause to that of equality of rights for women has a particular appeal to those who define the latter as a limited number of specific issues like education, jobs, pay, pensions, credit, and spousal rights. The ERA can do little more for us on those matters than we have already achieved by legislation and favorable judicial rulings, the argument goes, and to pursue the fight for an ERA in order to gain only marginal benefits involves heavy costs. But from a different point of view, "equality of rights under the law" is seen as a concept with national significance more akin to due process than to any bundle of identifiable constraints and requirements. For example, Representative Barbara Mikulski, Democrat of Maryland, a dedicated ERA partisan, likens the step-by-step, place-by-place approach to the freeing of slaves "plantation by planta-

---

20. 247 U.S. 251 (1918).
21. *New York Times,* January 9, 1937.
22. *United States Statutes at Large,* vol. 52 (GPO, 1938), p. 1067.
23. *United States* v. *Darby,* 312 U.S. 100 (1941).

tion."[24] Who knows how many plantations there are? Thomas Emerson, constitutional scholar and senior coauthor of an exhaustive analysis of the constitutional basis of equal rights for women, also equates the ERA with expressions of fundamental principle appropriate for the Constitution:

> Most of the cherished provisions of the bill of rights are expressed in the form of a general principle embodying a fundamental value of our society. Had the approach of the ERA opponents prevailed we would not now have in our Constitution provisions securing such basic rights as freedom of speech and of the press, freedom of religion, equal protection of the laws, and the right to due process of law.[25]

If, through the years, ERA's sponsors insisted on constitutional change as necessary to meet their objective, they have nevertheless held that the Supreme Court could effect such change without a formal amendment. According to Martha Griffiths, an appropriate interpretation of the equal protection clause would hold sex to be a suspect classification. Griffiths makes no secret of her impatience with the Court's reluctance to afford sex the same protection it affords race and alienage. But the Court has had the chance to reach that finding and backed away from it, so that what Vose terms the "most distinctive and dramatic technique of constitutional change in this century"[26] —Supreme Court reversals of previous positions—offers the only alternative to formal amendment that would lead the women's movement generally to accept the proposition that the battle had been won. If sex were suspect, any sex-based classification would be subject to "close judicial scrutiny," virtually an automatic death sentence for any classification under challenge. Even before she succeeded in moving the ERA through the House, Martha Griffiths testified that there would be no difference between an ERA and the equal protection clause of the Fourteenth Amendment "except that the Supreme Court has never found a law which discriminated on the basis of sex to violate the equal protection clause. . . . Had the Supreme Court applied the equal protection clause to women, this [amendment] would not be necessary."[27]

24. *Congressional Record,* daily edition (July 14, 1982), p. H4071.
25. Ibid. (November 8, 1983), p. E5365.
26. *Constitutional Change,* p. xxiii.
27. *Equal Rights for Men and Women, 1971,* Hearings before Subcommittee No. 4 of the House Judiciary Committee, 92 Cong. 1 sess. (GPO, 1971), pp. 46, 50.

Fourteen months after congressional passage of the ERA, with the proposal already ratified by thirty states and apparently on its way to easy success, four members of the Court were ready to short-circuit the ratification process as an earlier Court had short-circuited it in the case of the seemingly lost child-labor amendment. In *Frontiero* v. *Richardson,* the question for decision was whether a difference in treatment between servicemen and servicewomen who claim a spouse as a dependent constitutes an unconstitutional discrimination against servicewomen in violation of the due process clause. A finding of unconstitutional discrimination could be based narrowly on the particular statutes in question or could be based broadly on the rationale that ERA supporters had long urged—that sex is a suspect classification. Justice Brennan, joined by three of his colleagues, took judicial notice of congressional passage of civil rights and equal pay legislation and of the ERA, actions he judged to support the suspect classification position:

> Thus, Congress itself has concluded that classifications based upon sex are inherently invidious, and this conclusion of a coequal branch of government is not without significance to the question presently under consideration.
>
> With these considerations in mind, we can only conclude that classifications based upon sex, like classifications based upon race, alienage, or national origin, are inherently suspect, and must therefore be subjected to strict judicial scrutiny.[28]

The Court had passed over more than one earlier chance to assert that position, thus inviting speculation that it was the movement of the ERA through Congress that stimulated a plurality to adopt a stance that no justice had enunciated when offered the opportunity previously—for example, in *Reed* v. *Reed,* a 1971 gender classification case.[29] But the *Frontiero* plurality was just that; the necessary fifth vote that would make judicial doctrine could not be secured. Three members of the Court—speaking through Justice Powell—held that since the ERA would resolve the question of suspect classification, the Court should not "unnecessarily" decide "sensitive issues of broad social and political importance at the very time they are under consideration within the prescribed constitutional processes." Justice Stewart concurred in the judgment, agreeing "that the statutes before us work an invidious discrimination in violation of the Constitution"

28. *Frontiero* v. *Richardson,* 411 U.S. 677 at 688 (1973).
29. 404 U.S. 71 (1971).

but without accepting either the reasoning of the plurality that classifications based on sex are suspect or that of his three colleagues who
felt that the pendency of the ERA precluded such a ruling.[30]

The suspect classification idea gives the Court trouble whether or
not an equal rights amendment is in the wings. "The law of suspect
classes is largely one of latent confusion," J. Harvie Wilkinson III has
written. A clerk for Justice Powell at the time of the *Frontiero*
decision, Wilkinson later called the concept of suspect classification
both highly arbitrary and badly confused: "In the hierarchy of suspect
and potentially suspect classes, there are angels and archangels, but for
no readily discernible or articulated reason. . . . The suspect class is
thus an unruly horse which the Court refuses to tame."[31]

Whether the explanation lies in the confusion of the suspect class
idea, or, as Professor Leo Kanowitz has suggested, in the failure of
Congress to signal that its passage of the ERA was not meant to
discourage the Court from eliminating all sex-based discrimination
on equal protection grounds,[32] the conclusion must be that equal
rights partisans cannot show the battle to have been won without a
formal amendment. The argument that the amendment has become
unnecessary could only be sustained if the Supreme Court forbade all
classifications based on sex. Not only has it failed to do so, but
subsequent to *Frontiero,* in several instances the Court has upheld
gender-based classifications that could not have been sustained had
there been an ERA.[33]

Under the best of conditions, judicial lawmaking as a surrogate for
a formal ERA has its critics. "The 14th amendment to the U.S.
Constitution, most frequently the basis for sex discrimination suits,
offers uneven and uncertain protection against sex bias," the United
States Commission on Civil Rights reported in 1981. "The standard
developed by the Supreme Court to judge such claims under the 14th

30. *Frontiero* v. *Richardson,* 411 U.S. at 692, 691. See the discussion of the case in
Bob Woodward and Scott Armstrong, *The Brethren: Inside the Supreme Court* (Simon
and Schuster, 1979), pp. 253–55.

31. "The Supreme Court, the Equal Protection Clause, and the Three Faces of
Constitutional Equality," *Virginia Law Review,* vol. 61 (June 1975), pp. 945, 977, 983.
Wilkinson was appointed to the U.S. Circuit Court of Appeals in 1984.

32. *Equal Rights 1970,* Hearings before the Senate Judiciary Committee, 91 Cong.
2 sess. (GPO, 1970), p. 165.

33. *Kahn* v. *Shevin,* 416 U.S. 351 (1974); *Schlesinger* v. *Ballard,* 419 U.S. 498 (1975).

amendment is unclear," the commission went on, "both to the Court itself and to other Federal and State courts."[34] Senator John Glenn argues for the timelessness and stability of an equal rights amendment.[35] And speaking on behalf of the House Judiciary Committee's favorable recommendation in 1971, a conservative Republican congressman, Charles E. Wiggins of California, made the most eloquent case for new language in the Constitution:

> The power exists under various constitutional provisions to end discrimination on the basis of sex in America wherever it may be found. That existing power is far broader than the limited thrust of the constitutional amendment before us.
>
> Some may oppose the amendment as unnecessary for this reason. But the Judiciary Committee was persuaded that there exists an emotional need based upon a moral imperative that our Constitution contain a statement of sexual equality.[36]

During the ten years of struggle over ratification of the ERA, partisans underestimated the extent to which objectives had been achieved by legislation and by judicial rulings in specific areas. But without the inclusion of sex in the suspect classification interpretation of equal protection, congressional sponsors remain wary of the proposition that "we really won." Explaining why they are not content to give the expired ERA a state funeral and proceed to other women's issues, legislators outdo one another in emphasizing that the formal amendment would have important benefits for women. "In the absence of this amendment," Senator John Chafee, Republican of Rhode Island, says, "discrimination goes on — in education, in employment, in the granting of credit and insurance, and in the receipt of benefits." According to Representative Patricia Schroeder: "It is economics. It is survival. Women have learned that equal rights translates into economics. Therein lies the reason why women will continue to fight fervently for the ERA." Representative Bernard Dwyer, New Jersey Democrat, contends that "congressional enactment of legislation addressing particular economic problems of women has been only partially effective." And Representative William J. Coyne, Pennsylvania Democrat, says that "we cannot rely on a

34. *The Equal Rights Amendment: Guaranteeing Equal Rights for Women Under the Constitution,* Clearinghouse Publication 68 (GPO, 1981), p. 24.
35. *Congressional Record,* daily edition (July 1, 1982), p. S7791.
36. Ibid., vol. 117 (1971), p. 35296.

hodge-podge of various State ERAs to remedy the economic injustice that is truly national in scope."[37]

Some ERA proponents think that all purposes of the ERA can be achieved without formal amendment. If and when that happens, like the prohibition on child labor, the outcome will be unmistakable and universally recognized. To this time, the loss of the ERA cannot be attributed to a widespread belief that in lieu approaches have made it superfluous.

Organizational Survival Needs

In her postmortem on the defeat of the ERA, Janet K. Boles suggests that a shift in the primary goal of the National Organization for Women may have preceded that defeat. Citing Anthony Downs and Peter Blau on succession of goals, and James March and Herbert Simon on the relation of means and end, Boles writes, "As an organization grows older, its officers often tend to place a greater emphasis on insuring its continued growth and survival and less emphasis on its purported goals." In the particular case of NOW and the ERA, she goes on, "the goal of the national campaign may have been organization building and maintenance, *not* ERA ratification." And, "as the most visible and widely acceptable single issue identified with feminism, the amendment may have become a means of goal attainment."[38]

Boles says that the ERA issue transformed the National Organization for Women (NOW) into a group with an impressive political capacity. Between 1980 and 1982, membership doubled to 210,000; during the first half of 1982, NOW raised $1 million a month. Spearheading the drive for the amendment, NOW used the troubled campaign as an instrument to shore up NOW. "As chances for ratification became more remote, the National Organization for Women was able to capture the issue for its own purposes of building a strong network of political activists."[39] The most extreme interpre-

---

37. Ibid., daily edition (July 14, 1982), pp. S8178, H4064, H4078, H4084.
38. "Building Support for the ERA: A Case of 'Too Much, Too Late,' " *PS* (Fall 1982), p. 576.
39. Ibid., p. 577.

tation of the argument would make loss of the ERA an unwitting consequence of the National Organization for Women's preoccupation with organizational survival in a competitive environment.

An untold number of groups and organizations formed to accommodate the interests of women newly active in the 1960s. Among those that endure, the clear leaders are NOW and two unexpected spin-offs, the Women's Equity Action League, and the National Women's Political Caucus. Although some differences on substantive issues and on political strategy clearly exist among them, the three compete within much the same pool for membership and for financial support.

Despite the danger to its primacy posed by the threat of competition, NOW has consistently chosen not to temper its argument in order to broaden its appeal. In the case of the formation of the Women's Equity Action League (WEAL) in 1967, some older women invited NOW to abandon or playdown its pro-choice goal—as Betty Friedan has put it, "to choose between them and the young on abortion."[40] The question could have been finessed by a young organization bent on survival, but NOW held to the conviction appropriate to the time that abortion and the ERA constituted the core issues of the women's movement. The resulting decision of the dissidents to form WEAL when NOW had only a few thousand members temporarily jeopardized NOW's prospects for growth. While emphasizing its misgivings about NOW's pro-choice stand, WEAL joined NOW as a junior partner in the ERA fight, thus acknowledging NOW's leadership role on that issue even for women who in other respects found NOW too unconventional.

The National Women's Political Caucus (NWPC), organized in 1971 by Betty Friedan, Bella Abzug, and others, was expected to reach a broader range of women than did NOW. Friedan anticipated the NWPC would reach some who had not even identified themselves as feminist. Decisions about substantive issues to pursue would be made by state and local groups whose sole shared purpose would be the maximum representation of women as candidates for and holders of political office. The NWPC, according to Maren Lockwood Carden, within a couple of years "was realizing its hopes of being an umbrella

40. *It Changed My Life* (Random House, 1976), p. 106.

organization for politically involved women whatever their race, religion, or political persuasion."[41]

Emulating NOW, the NWPC also opened a Washington legislative office and began national lobbying activity in 1973. Soon thereafter, both organizations were in trouble, particularly hard hit, as Anne Costain has shown, by their memberships' anger over developments associated with national lobbying.[42] State and local resistance, manifested even in the withholding of dues to the national caucus, persuaded the NWPC to back away from national issues and to concentrate on election and appointment of women to public office. In the mid-1970s, NOW shucked off opponents of an intensified campaign for the ERA, while the NWPC tended to shy away from national activity on behalf of the ERA. Once those divergent judgments were implemented, NOW's growth, influence, and visibility steadily outstripped those of the NWPC. As time ran out on the ERA in 1982, the NWPC again took an unabashedly aggressive stand on behalf of the proposal. That activity was at once recognition of the primacy of the equal rights amendment among women's issues and acknowledgment that no women's group could avoid an ERA focus without jeopardizing its future.

If the hypothesis that NOW's own welfare displaced the ERA as its primary goal is to be sustained, NOW must be shown to have diverted its energies and resources away from ratification activity and toward alternative uses not particularly relevant to ratification. Ironically, some women activists who believe that NOW did not follow this course do believe that such a course would have been of more help to the movement than continued efforts to achieve ratification of an amendment they deem of marginal value. But no evidence has been put forward to show the deliberate displacement of the ERA goal. The organization did use the idea that ERA ratification was within sight and could be accomplished as a means of expanding its membership and raising money. Doing so itself helped sustain the momentum of the ratification campaign as much as it helped NOW's growth. If

41. *The New Feminist Movement* (Russell Sage Foundation, 1974), p. 139.
42. "Representing Women: The Transition from Social Movement to Interest Group," and "The Struggle for a National Women's Lobby: Organizing a Diffuse Interest," *Western Political Quarterly,* vol. 34 (March 1981), pp. 100–13, and vol. 33 (December 1980), pp. 476–91.

NOW had not been able to show membership growth and budget increases during the ratification drive, ERA opponents in unratified states could justifiably have claimed that support was softening in the face of opposition arguments. Displacement of its goal is not to be assumed because the organization strengthened itself at the height of a crisis for its program objectives.

In the tradition of all social-policy pressure groups, NOW finds its numbers and dollars growing or shrinking according to the rise and fall of popular belief in its effectiveness. Most social-policy interest groups starve until it can be shown that they can effect change. Successful causes—like those that abortion-rights groups are pressing—are often threatened with starvation as their socially concerned constituents record the win and turn to new causes. The important growth phase for a social-policy pressure group comes after it is taken seriously by the media and by politicians and before its stated objectives are achieved. If the objectives are not achieved in a reasonable period of time, it is once again not taken seriously—the fate of the National Woman's party. Repeated failure to achieve stated objectives discourages constituents and also leads to a falling off of support.

The quick and virtually uninterrupted run of ERA successes in Congress and the states between 1970 and 1974 did not dramatically swell NOW's fisc. Passage and ratification looked both easy and costless, as Martha Griffiths handled passage and ratification handled itself. But after 1975, prospects dimmed. Extension came neither easily nor without cost. An appeal for help made sense to ERA proponents who joined and contributed to NOW in hopes of capturing the elusive three states needed to ratify the proposal. As a result, NOW grew. Its ratification strategy may have been unwise or injudicious, but it did pursue the ratification objective. That it was able to do so with more rather than less money and more rather than fewer members does not demonstrate a shift in primary purpose away from enacting ERA in favor of sustaining NOW.

If NOW lost the battle for the ERA because of a preoccupation with organizational survival, it was not because the life of the organization became more important than the cause, but because the organization and the cause became virtually inseparable. Steady dedication to enactment of an ERA made NOW queen of the women's movement. There is no good evidence that the queen forgot her own history.

Frightened Women

Inequality between the sexes may be deemed indefensible by a large segment of the American population, but "equality of rights" by constitutional fiat may be feared lest it jeopardize the security that many middle-class, middle-aged women believe they enjoy under existing arrangements. "There remains a very large part of the female population," Professor Philip Kurland warned a Senate committee in 1970, "on whom the imposition of such a constitutional standard [of absolute equality] would be disastrous."[43]

If an ERA promises younger women an assured opportunity to compete for educational benefits, employment, and compensation on an equal footing with men, the argument continues, it promises nothing but trouble for women who are too old to be trained as doctors or lawyers or accountants, lack significant work experience, and have no financial resources other than those acquired and controlled by their husbands. The desire to open opportunities to some, Kurland counseled, should not be satisfied at the cost of removal of legal protections from others. Like the trade union women of yesteryear who resisted the loss of protective labor legislation, in Kurland's view mid-life women of the 1970s were well advised to resist the loss of what he perceived to be protections traditionally accorded American housewives.

Ten years later, with the ERA nearly interred, Andrew Hacker's postmortems picked up Kurland's theme: "Women opposed the ERA because it jeopardized a way of life they had entered in good faith." And, according to Hacker, that opposition is what did it in. Hacker suggests that "few men cared much either way.... A crucial reason for ERA's defeat was opposition from women" who feared the consequences of an ERA on divorce settlements and other protections available to housewives.[44]

If this view is correct, the opposition women involved conducted a remarkable underground campaign. Once the ERA was sent to the states for ratification, the cause was pursued by, among other groups, a united AFL-CIO, the National Organization for Women, the Na-

43. *Equal Rights 1970,* Hearings, p. 91.
44. "ERA-RIP," *Harper's* (September 1980), pp. 10, 14.

tional Federation of Business and Professional Women's Clubs, the General Federation of Women's Clubs, and Presbyterian, Baptist, Methodist, and Jewish federations, groups accurately described as from the mainstream of American life. The ERAmerica, a national alliance of over two hundred organizations that supported ERA, included the American Bar Association, the Girl Scouts, and the National Council of Senior Citizens. By the early 1970s, "with occasional exceptions," Irene Murphy has written, "religious groups, social welfare groups, occupational and professional associations, caucuses within professional and other groups agreed that the Equal Rights Amendment should be passed, and subsequently implemented by Congress and state legislatures."[45]

As for housewives committed to traditional roles, survey data consistently show them to have favored the ERA. The review of those data by Daniels, Darcy, and Westphal concludes that opponents did not represent the views of most housewives, that "only a minority of them actually opposed the amendment." Even in 1980, when he reported opposition among housewives at a high of 35 percent, Gallup showed 43 percent to favor the ERA.[46]

To the extent that women manifested forthright opposition to the ERA, they did so through Phyllis Schlafly's STOP ERA, "a single-purpose association of people . . . [that] doesn't stand for anything except the defeat of the equal rights amendment." Schlafly declines to explain the composition of the organization other than that "it is a voluntary association of women who are opposed to the equal rights amendment."[47] If STOP ERA represented women not avid for careers or for whom that option appears to come too late—according to Hacker, the women to whom state legislators finally listened[48]— Schlafly catered to them surprisingly little. "We oppose the equal rights amendment," Schlafly has explained, "because we are for women's rights." Pressed for details, Schlafly is more likely to cite other rights than a right to economic dependency: "I speak for

45. *Public Policy on the Status of Women* (D.C. Heath, 1973), p. 6.
46. Daniels, Darcy, and Westphal, "The ERA Won," p. 580; *Gallup Opinion Index*, no. 178 (June 1980).
47. *Equal Rights Amendment Extension*, Hearings before the Subcommittee on Civil and Constitutional Rights of the House Judiciary Committee, 95 Cong. 2 sess. (GPO, 1978), pp. 250–51.
48. "ERA-RIP," p. 14.

women's rights—the rights that women will lose if the equal rights amendment is ratified, such as the right of women to be exempt from the draft and military combat duty, to name only one." And, in an enumeration, economic dependency takes only third place:

> I feel that I speak for women's rights; the rights to have the laws which exempt women from military combat duty, the right to have the draft laws exclude women from induction, the right to have laws which say that the husband is liable for the support of his wife, the right to have single sex schools and colleges and various other differences that reasonable people may want in the difference of treatment between men and women.[49]

Inclusion of women under selective service and the use of women in combat duty are serious questions that have engaged the attention of constitutionalists, feminists, and politicians for years. Expressions of concern that an ERA might result in women in combat can more readily be found among men than among women. That objection to the ERA, made frequently by Schlafly, can hardly be related to Hacker's judgment that "women opposed the ERA because it jeopardized a way of life they had entered in good faith." The dependent housewives to whom Hacker refers are not in jeopardy of the draft, or of combat duty. They can have only an academic interest in the continuation of single-sex colleges and seem unlikely to be personally concerned about sex-segregated prisons, a phenomenon irrelevant to a way of life they entered in good faith.

A Census Bureau report published in September 1981, at the peak of the last push for ERA ratification, provided little comfort to any women who may have fought the ERA lest it have adverse effects on alimony awards. They had already lost. Very few of the women eligible for alimony or maintenance payments were awarded them:

> Of the 14.3 million ever-divorced or separated women in spring 1979, about 2 million (14 percent) were awarded or had an agreement to receive alimony or maintenance payments. . . . About 760,000, or slightly over one-third of the women awarded payments were supposed to receive them in 1978. However, only about 41 percent of these women received the full amount of payment that they were due, 28 percent received partial payment, and a similar proportion received no payment at all. The mean amount of alimony or maintenance for women receiving payments in 1978 was $2,850, or about 26 percent of their mean total money income.[50]

49. *Equal Rights Amendment Extension,* House Hearings, pp. 248, 255.
50. U.S. Bureau of the Census, *Current Population Reports,* Special Studies, series P-23, no. 112, *Child Support and Alimony: 1978* (GPO, 1981), p. 2.

Whoever or whatever killed the ERA, it could not have been frightened housewives determined to assure themselves of alimony or separate maintenance payments in case of divorce or separation. As a practical matter, alimony is not a common incidence of divorce.[51] Any woman who by the end of the 1970s still believed marriage to mean a permanent guarantee of support would have been so out of touch with reality as to cast doubt on her credibility as a lobbyist.

New Factors?

The inability to pass an ERA through Congress before 1972 had dual causes—the absence of a strong women's movement to provide organized group support and the simultaneous presence of firm opposition from organized labor. With the emergence of the new women's movement in the 1960s, enough group support developed to move Congress even as labor slowly reviewed the continuing validity of its position. A great wave of states ratified the proposal before the AFL-CIO worked its way to formal endorsement. Labor's conversion then further strengthened the cause.

Since Congress proposed the amendment in 1972, however, no accretive body of research data or experience has shifted the weight of evidence against an ERA. The potential upset of gender-related insurance-premium differentials and pay differentials, the probable end of alimony and other female-support awards as well as of draft deferments for women, the need to reconsider maternal preference in child custody, the haunting specter of unisex public restrooms— indeed, all of the consequential and the trivial arguments against an ERA—had been advanced and were well known before 1972.

Organized opposition seemed late to surface, the justifications for it old hat. The Reverend Jerry Falwell's 1981 explanation to an interviewer borrows heavily from the argument made by Senator Sam Ervin in 1972—an argument overwhelmingly rejected at that time by the Senate. The language of the amendment "is very ambiguous," Falwell complained, adding that "another problem is that women in America . . . would at some point in time, be forced into combat."[52]

---

51. Harry D. Krause, *Family Law in a Nutshell* (West Publishing, 1977), p. 331.
52. *Congressional Record*, daily edition (February 23, 1981), p. E622.

President Reagan's case against the ERA included a concern that it might weaken "labor relations and so forth that are definitely there for the benefit of women," a position that both the Women's Bureau of the Department of Labor and the AFL-CIO had long since abandoned. Reagan's opposition has seemed more perfunctory than spirited—a preference for statutory over constitutional change and for state action over federal. Having tried the constitutional approach and not been successful, Reagan says, why not try the statutory approach? And why not cleanse state as well as federal statutes of discriminatory provisions?[53] In any event, this president's indifference probably made little difference to an already stalled ratification effort. Since there once were plenty of votes for passage in Congress, but ultimately not enough affirmative votes in the state legislatures to meet the constitutional requirement, an explanation of the outcome should look to circumstances not present during congressional consideration or during the initial wave of ratifications.

The one detectable new ingredient subsequent to congressional action was the Supreme Court's decision in January 1973 decriminalizing nearly all abortions. Although the argument over decriminalizing abortion was a heated argument in the 1960s, ERA sponsors had insisted all along that their proposals would not bear on the abortion dispute one way or another. The *Roe* v. *Wade*[54] decision should have neutralized any suggestion put forward by opponents that an ERA might be read to overturn existing prohibitions on abortion. *Roe* overturned those prohibitions, thereby giving abortion the constitutional protection that an equal rights amendment would neither augment nor diminish. Because the decision was handed down while the ERA was pending, the effect was to give judicial credence to the independence of abortion from the ERA as a constitutional issue.

Antiabortion forces had not anticipated the kind of sweeping libralization of abortion mandated by *Roe* v. *Wade.* Their reaction was to press for a constitutional amendment to overrule the court, to test for constitutionally acceptable ways to limit abortion, and to oppose anything that might be construed as reinforcing the *Roe* doctrine. Not a dominant political force, antiabortion groups nonetheless are formidable. If they decided that an ERA would be inconsis-

53. *Weekly Compilation of Presidential Documents* (August 29, 1983), p. 1166.
54. 410 U.S. 113 (1973).

tent with their goals, and enlisted on the opposition side, that side gained significant additional strength. Neither opponents nor supporters of ERA could have done anything about *Roe,* but the possibility that the abortion dispute critically affected ERA ratification thus becomes a promising lead.

Chapter Three

Unanticipated Complications

THE EQUAL RIGHTS AMENDMENT had been debated sporadically for half a century and intensely for half a decade before final action on it by Congress in March 1972. Objections from activists and scholars invariably pinpointed the potential loss of special privileges accorded women rather than any addition to rights accorded them.

One example is a 1946 joint statement issued by ten national women leaders, headed by Eleanor Roosevelt and Frances Perkins. They complained that the amendment would wipe out both state protective legislation for women and women's advantages under social security, veterans' benefits, and workmen's compensation laws. "'Equal rights,'" the statement read, "is a deceptive slogan."[1] Similarly, three liberal congresswomen issued a declaration that warned the ERA would cause "chaos. . . . It will make it possible to wipe out the legislation which has been enacted in many states for the special needs of women in industry."[2]

That same year, a statement drafted by Professor Paul Freund of Harvard Law School and endorsed by deans and professors of twenty-one leading law schools—including such luminaries as Roscoe Pound of Harvard, Walter Gellhorn of Columbia, Willard Hurst of Wisconsin, Harry Shulman of Yale, and Blythe Stason of Michigan—viewed with alarm the range of provisions "dealing with the manifold relations of women in society [that] would be forced to run the gauntlet of attack on constitutional grounds" if an ERA were enacted. Certain to be subjects of litigation, these experts declared, were legal provisions benefiting women that dealt with a widow's allowance, the

1. *Congressional Record,* vol. 92 (1946), p. 9401. Other signers were Virginia Gildersleeve, Carrie Chapman Catt, Susan B. Anthony II, Anna Lord Straus, Mary Anderson, Mary McLeod Bethune, Rose Schneiderman, and Cornelia Bryce Pinchot.
2. Ibid. The congresswomen were Helen Gahagan Douglas (Democrat, California), Chase Going Woodhouse (Democrat, Connecticut), and Emily Taft Douglas (Democrat, Illinois).

obligation of family support and grounds for divorce, the age of majority and the right of annulment of marriages, and the maximum hours of labor for women in protected industries.[3]

During the two years of congressional consideration before passage in 1972, the heart of the case made against an ERA involved the amendment's consequences for protective labor legislation and for the traditional exemption of women from compulsory military service, particularly combat service. An opponent disposed to literal interpretation of the Constitution developed a litany of so-called terrifying consequences that included the predicted nullification of laws that exempted or excluded women from arduous and hazardous activities, both civilian and military; imposed on husbands the primary responsibility for support of their wives and children; undertook to better the economic position of women by, for example, fixing minimum wages for women in many states that had no minimum wage laws for men; and required separate restrooms in public buildings and public schools, or countenanced non-coeducational institutions of learning.[4]

Most members of Congress found the "terrifying consequences" either not so terrifying or not likely. Protective labor legislation and non-coeducational schools were disappearing without regard to enactment of an ERA; court enforcement of a husband's responsibility to support his wife and children already took into account the financial condition, earning capacity, and other circumstances of either spouse that affected the discharge of the obligation; the "threat" to separate prisons and separate restrooms was dismissed as a frivolous objection not worthy of elevation to the level of a serious question. Once organized labor began to abandon protective labor legislation, disputes over the ERA's potential consequences centered on the merits of drafting women and sending women into actual combat. In 1971 and 1972, legislators found it easy to beg the question. It was not then necessary either to provide a draft exemption and a combat exemption for women, or to affirm a sex-blind draft and the assignment of women to combat. Military service was voluntary. American forces were disengaging from combat. Adoption of an ERA would not alter

3. Ibid., p. 8018. Professor Freund's analysis was cited by congressional opponents of the ERA for the ensuing twenty-five years.
4. Ibid., vol. 116 (1970), pp. 29668–73.

any military service responsibilities then in effect. And even if it did, not many politicians wanted to argue with the general principle enunciated by Representative Shirley Chisholm, Democrat of New York: "Each sex, I believe, should be liable when necessary to serve and defend this country."[5]

After finally winning their battle in Congress, proponents foresaw no trouble in accomplishing ratification. The handful of diehards who had voted no in the House and Senate represented no known constituency. The metamorphosis of the liberal-labor opposition into the liberal-labor coalition in support of the ERA was all but complete, awaiting only pro forma action by the AFL-CIO convention. If faint stirrings could be heard of a new opposition that would adapt for nonworking women the "protection" theme discarded by working women, no stop-ERA movement worthy of the name had organized.

Despite these rosy circumstances, a careful vote-counter would have observed that the march to ratification inevitably would be slowed by peculiarities stemming from the date of final congressional action. Twenty-nine state legislatures were or would be in regular session between March 22, 1972, and the end of the year. An additional four legislatures were already in extra or special session on March 22, 1972. Barring the calling of special sessions elsewhere solely to consider ERA ratification—an expensive, unlikely eventuality—the proposal could be ratified by a maximum of thirty-three states in 1972. Since ratification required the approval of thirty-eight states, for all practical purposes it could not be achieved in 1972, but would carry over into 1973 when every state legislature, save that of Kentucky, would be in regular session. Without a single opposition voice necessarily being raised, the ERA's momentum was automatically slowed. There was time for organized opposition to form and develop.

If every state legislature had been in session between March 22, 1972, and, say, November 30, 1972, the equal rights amendment might have swept to ratification. Observe how very well the first eight months went for its supporters. Within forty-eight hours of congressional passage, six states ratified the ERA—more states than had ratified the child labor amendment in the first eighteen months after its passage. Within one month, fifteen states ratified; within two

5. Ibid., p. 28029.

months, eighteen; and by Thanksgiving 1972, eight months following passage, the total grew to twenty-two, a pace comparable to that of ratification of the woman suffrage amendment. Each of the four legislatures in special session in 1972 acted favorably, as did eighteen of the twenty-nine in regular session—a count that probably does not do justice to the ERA's strength in that the twenty-nine states included three that did not ratify women's suffrage until 1969, 1970, or 1984. Moreover, twenty-one of the twenty-two ratifications in those first eight months were achieved with at least a two-thirds majority in both legislative chambers of the various states involved.

Eight more states ratified between the following January and March 22, 1973, the first anniversary of congressional action. But if early 1973 represented the first possible opportunity for six of the eight to act because their legislatures had not been in session during the latter part of 1972, more than predetermined dates for convening and adjourning state legislative sessions now seemed to slow ratification. Cassandras sounded grim forebodings. "The momentum for passage of the amendment has sort of worn out," said the executive director of the National Women's Political Caucus in January 1973, "because it has already gone through in most of the states where it was a natural. Also, it's going to be tougher to get the last 16 states we need because there's a natural backlash setting in towards the gains that women are making."[6]

Both explanations are unconvincing, but both predictions were correct: momentum had "sort of worn out," and ratification did become "tougher." Two-thirds majorities were no longer to be achieved routinely; just four of the eight additions in 1973 came by two-thirds votes. As for momentum, although the legislatures in all twenty states that had not already ratified met some time in 1973, no state ratified that year after March 22. Because subsequent ratifications came so hard—three in 1974, one in 1975, and one two days before Jimmy Carter's inauguration in 1977—supporters eventually worked for and achieved an extension of time beyond the seven years originally provided.

No state ratified during the thirty-nine month extention. What in 1972 appeared to be a clear path to ratification was complicated in subsequent years by unforeseen events linked to the ERA by ties that

6. *New York Times*, January 15, 1973.

range from peripheral to distant to totally indirect. Each, however, contributed strength to what began as lackluster opposition.

Emergence of Opposition

Aside from a few constitutional lawyers who foresaw endless litigation and a few diehard labor officials who thought protective legislation still lived, opponents of an ERA were hard to come by when Congress was completing action on the proposed amendment. But politics abhors the absence of opposition; by the spring of 1972 a self-styled people's opposition appeared. Its spokesmen, comforted by a review of the fifty state legislatures' dates for convening, knew they had time to organize at the state level throughout 1972 without fear that the question might suddenly become moot. They were hard put, however, in view of the huge congressional majorities in favor of the ERA, to find a basis for opposition that might have appeal widespread enough to preclude ratification. The labor union women who continued to deplore the possible loss of whatever was left of protective labor legislation knew that issue to be of little interest to nonworking, middle-class housewives. The latter might find the possible loss of a husband's support responsibility more troublesome than the loss of protective labor legislation, but an opposition campaign that emphasized the male's support responsibility was unlikely to attract working women who did not enjoy it in the first place. In either case, invoking one or another "take-away" suggests only a crass defense of self-interest, rather than the humanitarian, patriotic, or other unselfish reason for opposition that might snowball.

With the 1973 state legislative season about to begin, opponents were still in search of a way to stop the forward march of the ERA to ratification. Even Phyllis Schlafly, who had lately emerged as leader of the opposition, was reluctant then to predict success for her side:

> If we get an adequate public debate whereby the issues were presented, I think it would be defeated. Getting that debate will require a lot of work and effort on the part of a lot of people, because the women's libbers are people who like to agitate and the women I deal with are not the kind who normally like to make themselves obnoxious. In addition, the business and professional women who are for the amendment can get time off to go and lobby, whereas women who are taking care of their husbands and families can't.[7]

7. Ibid.

Schlafly attacked the ERA on the grounds that it would abrogate support laws and would subject women to the draft. While the loss of draft exemption qualified as one more take-away argument, it also introduced a patriotic reason for opposition to constitutional equality: a vision of "weak" women forced into military and combat service with resultant disastrous consequences for the strength of America's armed forces. Women who supported ratification argued as Shirley Chisholm had earlier argued that participation in the defense of the country should be considered a privilege to be shared by all healthy Americans, not a burden to be thrust only on men. Opponents preferred to recall a Department of Defense communication about the ERA in March 1972 that suggested "that assigning men and women together in the field in direct combat roles might adversely affect the efficiency and discipline of our forces."[8]

But with the disengagement from Vietnam finally in sight, combat service for anyone receded from popular concern. In January 1973 the truce was signed, and Defense Secretary Laird terminated the military draft six months ahead of schedule. The announcement all but mooted military service as an ERA issue for the time being. Registration of men would continue just for the life of the statute. Consequently, the most severe threat posed by even a ratified and eventually effective ERA was that it might be construed to compel registration of women—but even that only in the unlikely event that the registration statute was subsequently renewed. The accident of timing that ended both American involvement in Vietnam and the draft in January 1973 made the specter of women in combat distinctly less useful to the ERA's opposition than would have been the case during the war years of the late 1960s when Americans were entering combat rather than withdrawing from it.

The claim that an ERA could lead to women in combat suffered a further decline in anxiety value in April 1975 as President Ford ended draft registration. By the end of the decade, when it would again break in their favor, ERA opponents had less need of the combat-service issue. Two unrelated events in 1973 and 1974, neither of them predictable, made the work of anti-ERA stalwarts easier and that of ratification proponents harder. One was the Supreme Court decision of January 1973 decriminalizing abortion. The second was an out-

8. *Congressional Record*, vol. 118 (1972), p. 9347.

burst of national admiration for Senator Sam Ervin stemming from his role as chairman of the Senate's Watergate hearings. Ironically, many ERA proponents—probably a substantial majority—looked favorably on the abortion decision, and an even larger proportion surely approved Senator Ervin's hearings. For every benefit, there is a cost.

Roe v. Wade

Abortion and the ERA were not commingled politically until after January 1973, when the Supreme Court in *Roe* v. *Wade* found a constitutional right to privacy to protect nearly all abortions.[9] The decision was quickly denounced and quickly applauded. Fervent opponents, including opponents who before had been largely indifferent to the ERA, were moved to take up arms against the proposed amendment lest its inclusion in the Constitution be understood to legitimize a judicial opinion they were determined at least to pare down, and preferably to overturn. Within ten days, seven senators, four of whom had voted for the ERA, prepared and introduced a constitutional amendment to overturn *Roe*.[10] On the other side of the issue and of the Capitol, Democratic Representative Bella Abzug of New York, an ERA stalwart, introduced legislation to eliminate any state laws of any nature concerning regulation of abortion.[11]

The lists that critics developed in the 1940s and 1950s of problems expected to be generated by an ERA are significant for their omission of the status of abortion law. Neither was it discussed in the 1970 colloquies critical of the ERA that Senator Sam Ervin engaged in either with Paul Freund of Harvard Law School or Philip Kurland of the University of Chicago Law School. United in opposition, the professors and the senator there review their perceptions of the troublesome constitutional issues that an ERA would engender.[12]

9. 410 U.S. 113 (1973).

10. S.J. Res. 119, 93 Cong. 1 sess., proposing an amendment to the Constitution of the United States for the protection of unborn children and other persons.

11. H.R. 254, 93 Cong. 1 sess. Abzug's remarks are in *Congressional Record*, vol. 119 (1973), pp. 1793–95.

12. *Equal Rights 1970*, Hearings before the Senate Judiciary Committee, 91 Cong. 2 sess. (Government Printing Office, 1970), pp. 72–103.

And if it might be said that in 1953 as in 1923, the decriminalization of abortion was not widely discussed, by 1970 the situation was quite different—abortion had become a public issue and a controversial one. Changes in abortion law were being argued state by state. Significantly, however, right through the final congressional debates on the ERA in 1972, opponents who insisted that it would invite intolerable litigation did not suggest the litigation would include a claim that the ERA carries with it the legalization of abortion.

Welcomed intellectually and emotionally by most groups sympathetic to the ERA, *Roe* was deplored by others—including some activists in the women's movement—who preferred to deal with the questions as politically separable. Political leaders who tried for years to push an ERA through Congress had no interest in introducing an abortion complication before the ERA was in place. They understood that equating an equal rights amendment with a liberalized abortion policy would not add to the strength of the former. No converts to the ERA are made in pro-choice circles, where a woman's freedom to choose or to reject abortion is upheld—members of those circles invariably have already declared for an ERA. The tricky problem is to secure or maintain allegiance to an ERA on the part of women and men opposed to liberalization of abortion. To do so requires that abortion and the ERA be treated as separate and distinct policy questions.

The initial instinct of the founders of the National Organization for Women was to favor separation. A plank favoring abortion was not even included in NOW's initial (1966) platform lest otherwise sympathetic Catholic women and conservative professional women be alienated from the equal rights idea.[13] A year later, however, the NOW convention modified that cautious posture with the addition of a separate proabortion plank. Betty Friedan's explanation of the "crisis of decision" implies that the conscience of the organization was at stake: "In actuality, the Equal Rights Amendment and abortion were and are the two gut issues of the women's movement essential to real security—and equality and human dignity—for all women, whether they work outside or inside the home."[14]

Because the planks were separately adopted, members of NOW

13. Betty Friedan, *It Changed My Life* (Random House, 1976), p. 84.
14. Ibid., p. 106.

who chose to could continue active support for the ERA and ignore abortion. Others, led by Dr. Elizabeth Boyer who had been an active recruiter for NOW in Cleveland, left the organization and founded the Women's Equity Action League, in effect a competitor group that declined to make repeal of abortion law part of its platform. "Dr. Boyer limited the organization's objectives to the attainment of equality through the full enforcement of existing laws, the passage of antidiscriminatory legislation, and the encouragement of girls to prepare for more rewarding jobs than they have in the past."[15] In fact, NOW and WEAL made common cause on employment issues and on the ERA. The formation of WEAL provided an organizational base for women who supported an ERA but could not be comfortable within a group that supported abortion. That made it possible for ERA sponsors in Congress to appeal for the votes of undecided and doubtful colleagues with continued assurances that a vote for ERA was not necessarily a vote for abortion, that determined support for the ERA existed even among activist women with apparently strong objections to abortion.

At a time when state abortion laws were subject to vigorous attack and enjoyed vigorous defense, the ERA was untainted by the dispute. The speeches of Phyllis Schlafly between March 22, 1972, and the end of that year worried about family support responsibility and women in combat, not abortion. A group called H.O.W. (Happiness of Womanhood) that claimed ten thousand members, and distributed pink buttons marked "I know H.O.W.," also organized against ratification, but its bill of particulars seemed no more detailed than the message on the button. In sum, before January 22, 1973, sponsors of the ERA purposefully denied that its inclusion in the Constitution would affect abortion law. Opponents made no claim to the contrary.

Nor did either side anticipate what potential consequences an upheaval in abortion policy might have for ratification of the ERA— probably because an upheaval appeared unlikely. Despite an evidently vigorous debate that resulted in liberalization of some state abortion laws in the 1960s and early 1970s, the overwhelming majority of those laws remained unchanged or changed only marginally.

15. Maren Lockwood Carden, *The New Feminist Movement* (Russell Sage Foundation, 1974), p. 135. See also Arlene Daniels, "W.E.A.L.: The Growth of a Feminist Organization," in Bernice Cummings and Victoria Schuck, eds., *Women Organizing* (Metuchen, N.J.: Scarecrow Press, 1979), pp. 133–51.

Before January 1973, pro-choice organizations in just four states had succeeded in effecting change approaching that mandated by the Supreme Court in *Roe*.[16] Who guessed that, at one fell swoop, the Court would wipe out restrictions on abortion in forty-six states? After *Roe*, it was pro-life groups—those convinced that abortion involves the impermissible taking of human life—that were forced to move into action. Pro-choice organizations, no longer forced to bang their heads against legislative and electoral stone walls, could fold their tents. Those organizations, to use John E. Jackson and Maris A. Vinovskis's characterization, were rendered nonessential: "With pro-life forces shocked by the Court decision and split on the exact wording of a proposal for a constitutional amendment, state-level pro-choice groups disbanded, victory seemingly achieved."[17]

Not all state-level pro-choice groups could have been used as core support for ERA ratification efforts in the states. In some cases, particularly if an earlier pro-choice mission had been carried out aggressively, that record might have been deemed a strategic liability for an ERA ratification role. In a few instances, the pro-choice groups were single-issue oriented and simply not available for a campaign on another issue. But if there had been clearer signs early in 1973 that ratification of the ERA was in jeopardy, its supporters would have been moved to preserve and inherit pro-choice organizations likely to be sympathetic and useful to the ERA in states where ratification appeared problematic. Instead, *Roe* simultaneously provided ERA's opponents a desperately needed additional issue and weakened ERA's supporters by leading to the dissolution of state-level organizations that eventually had to be replicated.

Before *Roe*, all of the argument over an ERA focused on women's inequality vis-à-vis men, and women's consequent need for legal protection—protection sought in constitutional form, Martha Griffiths insisted, only because the judiciary had failed to provide it. *Roe* introduced a new issue—the consequences of the instant new right it gave women to be rid of an unwanted fetus. The most significant aspect of that right, John Hart Ely quickly pointed out in the *Yale Law*

16. Alaska, Hawaii, New York, and Washington.
17. "Public Opinion, Elections, and the 'Single-Issue' Issue," in Gilbert Y. Steiner, ed., *The Abortion Dispute and the American System* (Brookings Institution, 1983), p. 73.

Journal, was that it was secured at the expense of fetuses, although the latter would seem to have an even more compelling claim than women to judicial protection as a minority unusually incapable of protecting themselves. "Compared with men, women may constitute such a 'minority;' compared with the unborn, they do not. I'm not sure I'd know a discrete and insular minority if I saw one, but confronted with a multiple choice question requiring me to designate (a) women or (b) fetuses as one, I'd expect no credit for the former answer."[18]

Ely's article suggested that an affirmation of women's rights could mean a rejection of any claimed rights of the unborn. As the abortion dispute grew in the wake of *Roe,* the armamentarium of the ERA opposition increasingly came to include opposition to abortion, and to benefit from the inclusion. "In heavily Catholic Illinois," Janet Boles concluded from her review of the lobbying campaign against ratification of the ERA in that state, "abortion has been a leading peripheral subject." Boles notes mailings sent in 1974 by opponents to church leaders in an attempt to link the ERA with the proabortion movement and quotes an ERA proponent that "conservative opponents [of the ERA] have been able to convince people that rights for women and rights for fetuses are incompatible."[19]

Those opponents who undertook to connect abortion and the ERA found their task simplified by NOW's belated determination to be out in front as protector of abortion rights. Repeal of abortion laws had become a formal NOW goal in 1967, yet for years it trailed behind the preeminent place reserved for the ERA in NOW's resolutions, issues, and goals. The organization's Task Force on National Legislation, for example, reported in October 1972 that its primary concern was the establishment of state coordination to facilitate state lobbying for the ERA. Nothing was said about facilitating state lobbying for repeal of abortion laws. The Task Force on State Legislation reported the collective number one goal for 1972 was passage of state ERAs,

18. "The Wages of Crying Wolf: A Comment on *Roe* v. *Wade,*" *Yale Law Journal,* vol. 82 (April 1973), pp. 920, 935. The "discrete and insular minority" reference is to a celebrated footnote in which Justice Stone suggested that the Court can give extraordinary constitutional protection to interests unable to form effective political alliances, hence "discrete and insular minorities." *United States* v. *Carolene Products Co.,* 304 U.S. 144 at 152, note 4 (1938).

19. *The Politics of the Equal Rights Amendment* (Longman, 1979), p. 107.

resolutions asking Congress to enact the federal ERA, and ratification of the ERA. The number two goal was repeal of abortion laws.[20]

If, for whatever reason—political strategy, membership preference, leadership preference, misperception of need, or some combination of these—NOW first seemed to give more weight to its ERA campaign than to its abortion plank, the balance changed for a time as the organization rushed to the protection of *Roe*. Beginning with a vigorous protest to the introduction of the constitutional amendment to reverse the *Roe* decision, NOW worked to fight off increasingly ingenious and persistent federal and state efforts to intrude on the freedom to abort that *Roe* had established. By the summer of 1973, NOW announced plans for a consumer boycott of seven companies that had declined to sponsor television reruns of two situation comedies with an abortion theme. Its hard line established, NOW subsequently moved to the forefront of opposition to all attempts to limit *Roe*'s applicability.

Phyllis Schlafly refers to "abortion-on-demand" as the "major antifamily objective of the women's liberation movement." That objective was satisfied, she has written, by a Supreme Court "so pro-abortion that it discovered an alleged right to abortion in the Four-teenth Amendment" although "such a right was clearly not intended by those who ratified the Fourteenth Amendment," nor "for 100 years" had anyone else seen a right to abortion there. Schlafly's implication that the Court still lacks a really respectable handle for its abortion decision is followed by her warning: "It will be easier to find the right to abortion in ERA."[21]

By 1975, a watershed year for the ERA, as the legislatures convened for full sessions in all seventeen states that had not already ratified the ERA, abortion qualified as an unhelpful complication. Schlafly cites two examples where a connection was made between the abortion decision and the ERA. The first was a telegram from a University of Texas law professor to Texas state legislators importuning them to rescind their earlier ratification:

> Ratification of the ERA will inevitably be interpreted by the Supreme Court of the United States as an explicit ratification and an approval by the

20. "Report of Task Force on National Legislation—October, 1972," and "Report of Task Force on State Legislation," in National Organization for Women, *Revolution: Tomorrow is NOW* (Washington: NOW, 1973).

21. *The Power of the Positive Woman* (New York: Jove/HBJ, 1977), p. 110.

people of the United States of its 1973 decision invalidating state anti-abortion statutes and of its declaration therein that the unborn child is not a human person whose life is protected by the Constitution.[22]

The second example, a letter from a Notre Dame law professor, was written some weeks before a ratification vote in the Indiana legislature:

> If the ERA were adopted, it would make clear beyond any doubt that the states would be disabled from prohibiting or even restricting abortion in any significant way. . . . I believe that the adoption of ERA would jeopardize, at least with respect to public institutions and personnel, the so-called conscience clauses which give hospitals and medical personnel the right to refuse on grounds of conscience to perform abortions.[23]

The "right of conscience," a proviso added to a federal health bill in 1973 as a congressional reaction to *Roe,* represented the earliest success of pro-life counterattacks to decriminalization of abortion. It both protected personnel and institutions receiving federal funds from being required to perform abortions in violation of their moral or religious beliefs and forbade employment discrimination against staff members who invoked the conscience clause. To say the ERA would put the clause in jeopardy was to tie the ERA directly to the proabortion side.

Early in 1973, a few months after *Roe,* a survey of chief executives of twenty-five proabortion organizations and twenty-five antiabortion groups included, inter alia, the question "Do you favor passage of the Equal Rights Amendment for Women?" In the proabortion groups, twenty-four of the twenty-five respondents favored passage of the ERA; in the antiabortion group, twenty of the twenty-five opposed passage of the ERA.[24] Of course, at the time the question was asked, *Roe* had made abortion a compelling issue. No one can be certain how the respondents might have reacted to the question before the liberalization of abortion became a reality.

---

22. Telegram from Professor Joseph Witherspoon, January 9, 1975, quoted in ibid. Witherspoon's views are detailed in "The Constitutional Concept of the Person and the Unborn Child," reprinted in *Proposed Constitutional Amendments on Abortion,* Hearings before the Subcommittee on Civil and Constitutional Rights of the House Judiciary Committee, 94 Cong. 2 sess. (GPO, 1976), pt. 1, pp. 12–30.

23. Letter from Professor Charles Rice, January 21, 1975, quoted in Schlafly, *Power of the Positive Woman,* p. 11.

24. Marilyn Falik, *Ideology and Abortion Policy Politics* (Praeger, 1983), p. 122.

A smoldering antagonism between NOW and the Catholic church—groups whose judgments about abortion could never be reconciled—broke open early in 1975. The ERA was not directly at issue, but its ratification prospects in such heavily Catholic states as Illinois, Missouri, and Louisiana dimmed further after the bishop of San Diego barred holy communion to any Catholic who admitted to membership in NOW or any other proabortion group. Hundreds of NOW members subsequently picketed the offices of the apostolic delegate in what was termed a mother's day of outrage against the church's support of antiabortion legislation.

In Congress, continued efforts to chip away at *Roe* included enactment of a prohibition on the use of foreign aid funds to perform abortions or coerce anyone into performing them, and proposals for riders on appropriations bills to ban the financing of abortions by medicaid. Such riders, offered and rejected in both 1974 and 1975, generated lobbying that served to publicize the overlaps between antiabortion activists and ERA opponents and between proabortion activists and ERA supporters. As a matter of strategy, ERA supporters had thought it politic to avoid publicizing those overlaps.

The year that proponents foresaw as the year of victory for the ERA, 1975, goes down instead as a year of disaster. It began with thirty-three states in the ratification fold and ended with thirty-four as North Dakota became the sole addition. Moreover, in outcomes that Phyllis Schlafly accurately describes as moving "the momentum all against the ERA," New York and New Jersey voters defeated— 1,950,993 to 1,470,213 and 860,061 to 828,290, respectively—proposed equal rights amendments to their state constitutions. The legislatures of both states had ratified the federal ERA in 1972. The state ERAs had been urged as a way to achieve the equal rights objective without waiting for ratification of the federal amendment and the subsequent two-year delay in its effective date. Instead, voters in two liberal states rejected that idea at just the moment of ERA's greatest need for support.

Phyllis Schlafly, who had been warning Catholics that the ERA would require the church to admit women to the priesthood and to abandon single-sex schools or lose tax exempt status, enrolled as a first-year law student in the fall of 1975. She and the STOP ERA drive had had indisputable success beginning in the spring of 1973, and through the ensuing two and a half years. In that time, only four states ratified, none by votes approaching the extraordinary majorities common in the first twelve months. A substantial part of the explanation lies in the accident of timing that made abortion policy a national issue during those crucial years. Another part of the explanation lies in a different accident of timing, this one involving an issue with no apparent ties to the ERA—the Watergate break-in and Senate hearings in 1973 and 1974 on that event.

Senator Ervin as "Legendary Man"

The surprisingly strong Senate vote of 84–8 for passage of the ERA in March 1972 was helped by President Nixon's forthright endorsement timed for release to the Senate by Republican leader Hugh Scott shortly before the roll call. Virtually all eight no votes came from the old guard, literally as well as figuratively—four from senators over the age of seventy, only one from a senator under fifty, James Buckley, the New York Conservative who was forty-nine. Of the two Democrats among the eight, both were over seventy, both were Senate veterans, both were southern conservatives with low marks from the liberal Americans for Democratic Action and high marks from the conservative Americans for Constitutional Action. One of the Democrats, Sam Ervin, had been leader of the Senate opposition to the ERA at least since the retirement of Carl Hayden, Democrat of Arizona, in 1969.

"North Carolina's senior Senator, Sam Ervin, Jr.," wrote the authors of the *Almanac of American Politics* in 1972, "is a persistent and articulate opponent of federal legislation and administrative action that, in his opinion, violates constitutional freedoms."[25] Ervin's explanation of his persistent and articulate opposition to the ERA in the pristine form in which it passed the House did not turn solely on the protection of constitutional freedoms, but also on what he viewed as the danger of obscurity in constitutional language:

> The word "sex" is imprecise in exact meaning, and no proposed constitutional amendment ever drafted exceeds the House-passed equal rights amendment in scrimpiness of context. The amendment contains no language to elucidate its meaning to legislators or to guide courts in interpreting it. When all is said, the House-passed equal rights amendment,

25. Michael Barone, Grant Ujifusa, and Douglas Matthews, *The Almanac of American Politics, 1972* (Boston: Gambit, 1972), p. 583.

if adopted, will place upon the Supreme Court the obligation to sail upon most tumultuous constitutional seas without chart or compass in quest of an undefined and unknown port.[26]

That argument, stated in 1970, and repeated in 1971 and 1972, seemed to be more persuasive to Senate colleagues when first advanced than in the subsequent years.[27] Witness the short shrift given in 1972 to Ervin's twenty-six pages of minority views and the overwhelming defeat of each of his nine proposed amendments to the "clean" ERA passed by the House. Ervin's concerns about constitutional language were not then widely shared. His various proposals to preserve state or federal laws granting women special treatment attracted a maximum of eighteen votes on the Senate floor. At the time Congress passed the ERA, proponents confidently dismissed Sam Ervin, Jr., as an engaging southern senator with anachronistic views of women's capacities and activities that came wrapped in expressions of fear for the Constitution. Their confidence seemed reasonable; only a cataclysmic event that gave him national stature as a protector of the Constitution could make Ervin's opposition to the ERA a consequential problem rather than a trivial annoyance—and the last real constitutional cataclysm dated to 1861.

The modern constitutional cataclysm came to pass. In May 1973 when the ERA lacked eight of the thirty-eight states required for ratification, the Senate Select Committee on Presidential Campaign Activities—the Watergate Committee—opened its public hearings with Senator Ervin as chairman. Without question, Ervin did quickly achieve national stature as a protector of the Constitution. By February 1974, when that year's *Almanac of American Politics* appeared, its authors added an admiring sentence to their earlier description of Ervin: "Today, because of his devotion to the Constitution, the Chairman of the Senate Watergate Committee has become a legendary man."[28] And a few years later when Ervin came out of retirement to testify against an extension of time for ERA ratification, the measure's chief Senate sponsor, Birch Bayh, greeted him as a constitu-

26. *Congressional Record,* vol. 116 (1970), p. 29670.
27. In 1970 the Senate adopted a limiting amendment; in 1971 the House Judiciary Committee adopted two limiting amendments, both subsequently rejected on the floor; in 1972 both the Senate Judiciary Committee and the full Senate rejected all limiting amendments.
28. Barone, Ujifusa, and Matthews, *Almanac of American Politics, 1974,* p. 739.

tional hero: "It gives me a little lump in my throat to have you back in this room where you really saved the Union."[29]

Exactly because he made his case against the ERA as a constitutionalist, Sam Ervin was the critic that the ERA could least afford to have elevated to the status of legendary man, savior of the Union, protector of the Constitution. And ERA proponents could least afford to have him so elevated in 1973–1974 when the opposition was most in need of issues and events that might impede ratification activity. Ervin's fame and number of outspoken admirers (who probably included most ERA supporters) grew steadily throughout 1973 and into 1974. How much did Ervin's negative views on the ERA, freely given in 1975 as before, contribute to the massacre of 1975 when legislators in no less than eight "possible" states rejected ratification? (Approval by four of them would have made the ERA the twenty-seventh amendment.) The question is unanswerable. What is certain is that the views of Ervin as constitutional hero figured far more significantly in the evolution of a climate of doubt, hesitation, and restraint nurtured by ERA's opposition than those same views had figured when Ervin was merely a small town constitutional lawyer in a Senate seat. As late as 1978, "If good old Senator Ervin is Against ERA, It Must Be Bad" showed up as one of thirteen "fancies" discussed in *The Equal Rights Handbook*.[30] No other individual or institutional opponent merited comparable recognition. The opposition of pre-Watergate Senator Ervin would not have either.

Afghanistan: The Draft Resumes

After the disappointing legislative season of 1975 when only North Dakota ratified, supporters became increasingly worried about the outlook for ultimate ratification of the ERA and increasingly interested in devising strategies to enhance its prospects. The strategies they devised qualify instead as self-inflicted wounds. The self-inflicted wounds are distinguishable, however, from those caused by the three accidents of timing over which neither ERA's proponents nor its

29. *Equal Rights Amendment Extension,* Hearings before the Subcommittee on the Constitution of the Senate Judiciary Committee, 95 Cong. 2 sess. (GPO, 1979), p. 182.

30. Riane Tennenhaus Eisler, *The Equal Rights Handbook* (New York: Avon, 1978), p. 28.

opponents had any control. The timing of *Roe* v. *Wade* and of Senator Ervin's Watergate hearings are two of the latter; the third is the Soviet invasion of Afghanistan, which reawakened old anxieties about drafting women and their role in combat.

In October 1978, as the climax of a campaign that began more than a year earlier, Congress voted the ERA a reprieve from March 1979 to June 1982. An immediate effect was to ease the pressure on what would otherwise have been a do-or-die ratification effort in the first months of 1979 when *die* seemed far more likely than *do.* The reprieve changed the odds on long-run success—1980 would be an election year; women could make candidates' interest in ratification a condition of support. If the three states still needed were not brought into camp during 1979 or before the election in 1980, a full state-legislative season in 1981 would provide another opportunity to get the job done—perhaps with newly chosen and more sympathetic legislators.

Prospects for success could honestly be thought to be improving. By granting the reprieve, Congress had reaffirmed support for an ERA. Although far from ended, the abortion dispute had lost some intensity as the Supreme Court in a series of 1977 cases involving public funding showed a degree of flexibility in abiding some state efforts to chip away at *Roe*.[31] Senator Ervin, now retired, was likely to be less well remembered and less revered as the years passed. The lobbying style of NOW had become more conventional and more effective as Eleanor Smeal, its president since 1977, made the ERA her great objective. Perhaps most important, a good part of the original opposition argument about alimony, dower rights, protective legislation, and the like was increasingly irrelevant, better suited to a different era than to that characterized by equal employment opportunity and two-earner households. What, asked rational proponents of the ERA, would debar only three states from ratifying the amendment in 1980 or 1981 and having it done? An answer they could not foresee was the return of an old trouble—equality in the military.

From the beginning, the controversial questions that divided ERA proponents and their opponents included whether women should be made subject to a draft, whether women should be exempted from

---

31. *Beal* v. *Doe,* 432 U.S. 438 (1977); *Maher* v. *Roe,* 432 U.S. 464 (1977); *Poelker* v. *Doe,* 432 U.S. 519 (1977).

combat roles, and how the ERA might affect the answers. Proponents put forth arguments like Shirley Chisholm's—that defense of democracy via military service should not be denied women, ERA or no, and that if the amendment assured equal access to that opportunity, so much the better. And most supporters insisted that the ERA no more mandated combat roles for women than any preexisting selective service statute mandated combat roles for all military personnel without regard to physical capability. Opponents, on the other hand, held that an ERA would effect an undesirable and undesired change in law and custom, subjecting women to the draft and to combat assignment on an equal basis with men.[32]

When the Soviets invaded Afghanistan in December 1979, the United States had gone six and a half years without a military draft, and more than four years without draft registration. During the years of an all-volunteer force, the armed services encouraged women to enlist, the service academies began to admit women, and virtually all noncombat military-occupation specialities became available to women. The percentage of women in the services had approximately quintupled from the 1.6 percent of 1973. It would have been appreciably higher if women had been entering the services as draftees, although no one knows what effect a sex-blind draft would have had on the actual distribution of military tasks between men and women.

Four years after the draft ended, Phyllis Schlafly still thought it useful in making her case against the ERA to include an extended warning about equality in the military. Turning the "no more war, no more draft" psychology into an attack on "the naivete of the ERA proponents who blithely assume that we have now achieved a utopia in which we will have no more wars and no more conscription," Schlafly claimed instead that "logic, history, and common sense teach us otherwise." Not only is there war and conscription in the future, but "ERA will require mothers to be drafted on exactly the same basis" as fathers, and "no matter how many there are, it is no step forward to require that half of our casualties be women."[33]

There is no gainsaying the problem the draft issue posed for the ERA. Schlafly is surely correct in asserting that there has been no

---

32. See, for example, the colloquy between Senator Ervin and Professor Philip Kurland in *Equal Rights 1970, Hearings*, p. 100; see also testimony of Admiral Thomas Moorer in *Equal Rights Amendment Extension, Senate Hearings*, pp. 341–54.

33. *Power of the Positive Woman*, pp. 125–26.

national demand for women to be sent into battle equally with men, although support for the equal conscription of women, growing even when she wrote in 1977, grew further by 1979–1980. (Not long thereafter, a majority of the population favored equality in conscription. Citing year-old survey data, Martin Binkin and Mark J. Eitelberg noted in November 1983 that "better than half of the general population—whether in favor of a draft now or only in the case of national emergency—support the conscription of women as well as men.")[34]

Proponents of an ERA derive maximum benefit from the absence of conscription. When there is no conscription, raising it as an issue can be dismissed as a smokescreen; claiming that an ERA would compel the drafting of women can be dismissed as speculation added to smokescreen; asserting that an ERA would force women draftees into combat can be dismissed as illogic atop speculation added to smokescreen. If there must be a draft, ERA supporters go on, the ERA would have no effect on it because Congress would include women— ERA or no. And women's combat participation will always be a function of physical capacity, not of an ERA. Opponents of the ERA frame it as a choice—either drafting women and sending them into combat, or exempting women from the draft and protecting them from combat. During most of the ratification years, world tensions and national affairs in military matters operated to the advantage of proponents. Since there was no draft, opponents could only conjure up a grim vision of the ERA's possible effect on a nonexistent statute.

President Carter's reaction to Afghanistan included a decision to resume registration, without actual conscription, under the Selective Service Act of 1948.[35] No funds had been requested or appropriated for that purpose since 1975. (The draft itself had been terminated in January 1973.) Congress greeted the idea unenthusiastically, many members reminding one another and their constituents of a negative judgment the selective service system rendered on the idea of premobilization registration. In any event, to the satisfaction of equal rights proponents at least, the president first asked for money to

34. "Women and Minorities in the All-Volunteer Force," paper prepared for a conference on "The All-Volunteer Force after a Decade: Retrospect and Prospect," U.S. Naval Academy, November 1983, p. 26.

35. "The State of the Union: Address delivered before a Joint Session of the Congress, January 23, 1980," *Public Papers of the Presidents: Jimmy Carter, 1980–81* (GPO, 1981), bk 1, p. 198.

register women as well as men.[36] As equal rights supporters had predicted, a gender-free selective service that did not depend on ratification of the ERA seemed to be unfolding. Therefore, ratification of the ERA would effect no change.

Both the House Armed Services Personnel Subcommittee and the Senate Armed Services Manpower and Personnel Subcommittee saw things differently. The former rejected registration of women (8–1) early in March 1980; the Senate subcommittee followed suit (5–2) six weeks later.[37] An amendment providing for registration of women that was offered on the House floor provoked hardly any rhetorical support, let alone votes. It went down on an unchallenged voice vote.[38] Subsequently, a lawsuit challenging Congress's male-only decision as impermissible discrimination against men failed to impress the Supreme Court. In June 1981 the Court held in *Rostker* v. *Goldberg* that since registration is designed to prepare for a draft of combat troops and women remained ineligible for combat, the sexes were not similarly situated for purposes of military service. Accordingly, no constitutional provision mandated similar treatment.[39]

Phyllis Schlafly could feel once again that her enemies had indeed been delivered into her hands. Here was today's reality in decisionmaking about military equality, and the public policy response did not provide even for registration of women, let alone equality in military assignments. Schlafly had insisted that equality in the military would be a radical change contrary to customs and mores, and to the wishes of the majority of citizens. The outcome of the 1980 draft-registration proposal seemed to bear her out on the latter point. Congress chose to reject equality in registration lest it lead to equality in conscription, perhaps in assignment, and plausibly in combat. Since everyone agreed Congress would not have comparable freedom under an equal rights amendment, the ERA could now be denounced as a blunderbuss that would produce undesired and undesirable effects. In Schlafly's graphic terms, "ERA would tie a constitutional noose around our necks for all future wars."[40]

36. *Congressional Quarterly Almanac, 1980*, p. 41; *Public Papers: Carter, 1980–81*, p. 333.
37. *Congressional Quarterly Almanac, 1980*, pp. 41, 43.
38. *Congressional Record*, daily edition (April 22, 1980), pp. H2728, H2747.
39. *Rostker* v. *Goldberg*, 453 U.S. 57 (1981).
40. *Power of the Positive Woman*, p. 121.

Understandably, given their different viewpoints, the decision in *Rostker* v. *Goldberg* left Eleanor Smeal and Phyllis Schlafly respectively depressed ("blatant discrimination") and ecstatic ("a tremendous victory"). Each of them understood the significance of *Rostker* for the ERA ratification drive, then about to enter its final do-or-die year. Throughout American history, Congress had always exempted women from compulsory military service, and the Court had now found no constitutional impediment to Congress's continuing to provide such exemption. But a preponderance of legal opinion held that an ERA would subject women to conscription, and that it might, depending on subsequent judicial interpretation, subject women to military combat. If the Court had interpreted the Constitution already to have fixed those same responsibilities on women, the military status of women would be unaffected by ratification of the ERA. One of the major stumbling blocks to ratification would have been eliminated. Instead, *Rostker* underscored Schlafly's argument that the ERA would involve "take-aways"—in this case, a take-away both of women's exemption from compulsory military service and of the right of Congress in its wisdom to provide for that exemption.

Smeal viewed with alarm what she termed the decision's "symbolism." Because of it, she predicted, a drift toward other discriminatory practices could be expected as the ideas implicit in the Court's opinion worked their way into such areas as discussions of lower wage scales for women.[41] Her antagonist, Phyllis Schlafly, kept her eye on the ERA, the immediate target:

> It's perfectly obvious that if ERA were in the Constitution, the decision would have gone the other way. I think this decision puts the nail in the coffin of ERA.
>
> We thank God the equal rights amendment is not in the Constitution, or else the Supreme Court would have been compelled to hold that women must be drafted any time men are drafted.[42]

Schlafly would seem to have the best of this argument. Justice William Rehnquist's opinion emphasized that the case arose in the context of Congress's authority over national defense and military affairs: "Perhaps in no other area has the Court accorded Congress greater deference."[43] Smeal's expressed anxiety about the effect of the

41. *New York Times,* June 26, 1981.
42. Ibid.
43. *Rostker* v. *Goldberg,* 453 U.S. at 64.

opinion on discussions of lower wage scales for women is simply unwarranted.

Smeal chose not to use the opportunity to urge ratification of the ERA as a way of countering the decision in *Rostker*. To have done so would clearly have been counterproductive. Insofar as they involved the fate of the ratification effort, the stakes were high in *Rostker*. Schlafly took the whole pot and she bragged about it. Smeal lost her bet and sought to divert her backers' attention to a different game. But players on both sides knew that the fate of the ERA now depended on persuading mostly southern state legislatures that they should ratify an amendment that was very likely to overturn an existing, judicially sustained exemption of women from combat and the draft. That was an argument with limited appeal, especially in the South.

An equal rights amendment to the United States Constitution can hardly have crossed the minds of the Soviet leaders who decided on an invasion of Afghanistan. Nor is it likely to have been given much thought by the Republican politicians who decided to steal their Democratic opponents' campaign plans. Even the drive to decriminalize abortion, while related to the idea of equal rights for women, ran along a different track. Separately and collectively, however, their timing created unanticipated complications with severe negative effects on the ratification of the ERA.

Chapter Four

Suspect Procedures

THE USE OF unconventional parliamentary techniques on behalf of constitutional change is incompatible with the cautious approach to formal alteration that has characterized American constitutionalism for two hundred years. Similarly, a nonnegotiable proposal is incompatible with the diversity of interests and the disposition to compromise that characterize Congress. But persuaded of the absolute justice of their position, sponsors of the equal rights amendment hold its unqualified language to be nonnegotiable, and they embrace unconventional techniques to advance it. Whether unconventional procedures, employed once to allow an extraordinary majority to work its will on an ERA, can be used again to sustain or to renew the amendment and its original language is problematic.

As a practical matter, when extraordinary procedures are resorted to in a legislative body, members must make dual judgments—one about the merits of the substantive question involved, another about the propriety of the procedure. The ERA survived intact as long as judgments about merit and procedure coincided. As negative judgments about procedural fairness intruded on consideration of the merits of an equal rights amendment, its prospects faded.

Extension

Ratification prospects for the ERA appeared bright on the first anniversary of congressional passage, possible on the second, uncertain on the third, doubtful on the fourth, and bleak on the fifth. Outraged by opponents who counseled "Hold out and the ERA will expire," supporters countered with an inspirational justification for more time: "It is going to be a cliffhanger, and human justice should not be a cliffhanger."[1] At that point, many supporters and most—but not all—congressional sponsors embraced a plan to extend the allowable period for ratification. Their untested theory held that the seven-year limit was not itself part of the language proposed for inclusion in the Constitution and therefore could be changed by ordinary congressional action.

Congress ultimately adopted an extension resolution, albeit cutting the stretch-out from an additional seven years to thirty-nine months.[2] A parade of constitutional lawyers from the nation's leading law schools differed over technical details but agreed on Congress's legal right to amend the "resolving clause" of the joint resolution it had long since passed and sent to the states. If Yale's Charles Black believed an extension required a two-thirds vote of each house, since the package as originally passed necessarily required that extraordinary majority, Yale's Thomas Emerson thought a two-thirds vote unnecessary since "it would have been perfectly proper for Congress to have two resolutions, one dealing with a mode of ratification, and one with the substantive provisions." Only the substantive provisions, Emerson argues, were intended by Article V to apply to the two-thirds vote. Again, in Black's opinion an extension resolution should be submitted to the president. While Emerson thinks "the general principle should be that you either have a two-thirds vote or a presidential signature," he concludes that is not what the Supreme Court has held.[3]

In the event, a two-thirds vote was not secured, nor was a formal requirement of presidential approval imposed. President Carter chose to sign the extension resolution anyway, thus making academic the argument between Yale academics that was joined albeit not broadened by leading lights from Harvard, Columbia, and Duke.[4]

Opponents of extension termed it an unfair procedure that changed the rules in the middle of the game. Most proponents of the extension apparently thought it to be the only hope for ratification, but some,

1. *Equal Rights Amendment Extension,* Hearings before the Subcommittee on Civil and Constitutional Rights of the House Judiciary Committee, 95 Cong. 2 sess. (Government Printing Office, 1978), p. 163.

2. H.J. Res. 638, 95 Cong. 2 sess. (1978).

3. *Equal Rights Amendment Extension,* House Hearings, p. 73.

4. Erwin Griswold (Harvard); Ruth Bader Ginsburg (Columbia); William Van Alstyne (Duke).

like Representative Robert McClory, an original sponsor of the ERA, argued that a shift of emphasis from ratification to extension would dilute the strength of proponents and diminish the prospects for ratification. Too gracious, perhaps, to say "I told you so," McClory, like others who had misgivings, wonders whether adoption of the extension strategy contributed to the death of the ERA by unnecessarily providing opponents an additional talking point.

The original seven-year limit was not perceived as problematic by pro-ERA legislators who, in 1970, 1971, and 1972, had more immediate concerns. During those years, first discharging the resolution from the House Judiciary Committee and later coping with Birch Bayh's uncertain availability as Senate floor manager because of his wife's critical illness preoccupied sponsors. Martha Griffiths, in any event, thought seven years "ample"—indeed, she believed that the amendment "would be ratified in less than 2 years." John Conyers, Jr., another Michigan Democrat and cosponsor, thought a time limit appropriate, and that "7 years ought to be long enough to know if we are going to get it through or not. If we cannot do it within 7 years, I find it very difficult to understand why we would need more time."[5] But leaders of the National Woman's party (NWP) predicted trouble. They insisted experience with the suffrage amendment showed "how the opponents of a constitutional amendment, by requesting studies, holding hearings, setting up special commissions, etc., can prevent ratification within a specified time." They predicted that a seven-year provision "would be a death blow to the amendment."[6]

The NWP correctly envisioned the outcome of the ratification effort, but it incorrectly presaged the effective use of time-consuming tactics. After rejecting the ERA several times, Indiana, in January 1977, became the last state to ratify—twenty-six months before the expiration of the seven years originally allowed and sixty-five months before the expiration of the extended period ultimately allowed. But ratifications did not end because votes could not be taken. Subsequent to the success in Indiana, repeated votes were taken in Illinois and in Florida, only to fail repeatedly in those states as the amendment had failed on votes in Nevada, North Carolina, South Carolina, Georgia, Virginia, and Oklahoma. Between 1972 and 1982, floor votes

5. *Equal Rights for Men and Women, 1971,* Hearings before Subcommittee no. 4 of the House Judiciary Committee, 92 Cong. 1 sess. (GPO, 1971), pp. 41, 48.
6. Statement of Margaret Ramey and Margery C. Leonard in ibid., p. 247.

were taken on the ERA in both chambers of forty-five state legislatures, and in one chamber of three more. Filibustering of one sort or
another by the opposition would not deserve an entry in a roster even
of improbable explanations for the loss of the ERA.

While opponents did not filibuster in the state legislatures to
preclude votes on ratification, they did take the seven-year provision
at face value. For Congress to vote an extension less than a year before
the proposed amendment would have expired seems unfair to opponents whose planning had been based on precluding favorable action
in fifteen states until March 1979. Strategy was designed and personnel deployed in the belief that they need not be used beyond that fixed
date. Erwin Griswold, a former Harvard Law School dean and a
former solicitor-general of the United States, once likened the added
time to "extending the time of a football game. . . . It might be after 14
minutes and 58 seconds in the final quarter with the score tied and
one team on the other's 1 yard line."[7] The implication, of course, was
that the character of both situations—sports contest and constitutional contest—would be changed by the unanticipated addition of
time.

Robert McClory of Illinois, who was principal Republican sponsor
of the ERA resolution in 1971, anticipated that a time extension
would open the way for irrelevant and prejudicial issues to be injected
into the ERA debate and thus weaken rather than strengthen the
prospects for ratification.[8] Procedural fairness itself became one of
those prejudicial issues, the appearance of diminished commitment
another. The questions of fairness and of weakened congressional
commitment were linked by those who regarded authorization to
rescind an act of ratification to be a proper quid pro quo for
authorization to ratify during an extension. Proponents of the amendment viewed rescission as a dangerous game, however, and beat it
down in both House and Senate.[9] Although the Senate approved
extension 60–36, the key vote on allowing states to rescind a previous
ratification during the extension period was much closer, 55–44.
Extension limped through the House, 233–189. The contrast could
hardly have been greater between the House of the early 1970s that

7. *Equal Rights Amendment Extension*, House Hearings, p. 112.
8. Ibid., p. 4.
9. *Congressional Record*, vol. 124 (1978), pp. 26257, 33355.

deplored Emanuel Celler's unfairness in barring a hearing for the ERA and rolled over his opposition, and the House of 1978 that squirmed uncomfortably over fairness in voting a time extension without attaching rescission authorization.

The extension problem pained many supporters and diminished the zeal of others. Some of the legitimacy that the ERA derived from virtually unanimous congressional support in 1972 was vitiated by the substantial vote against extension—a vote interpreted to mean that many congressmen now had doubts about an ERA. Among original enthusiasts like McClory, whose legal, ethical, or political judgments pointed away from a time extension, some suppressed such judgments, others quietly retired from the fight for ratification. No state ratified during the additional thirty-nine months, so there was no gain. To ascribe loss of the ERA to the extension strategy, however, demands a showing that states prepared to ratify before the original deadline pulled back because of the extension. That case simply cannot be made. Nothing changed. Had there not been an extension, the proposal would just as surely have expired, three states shy of ratification, in March 1979. No reluctant state gave an indication that it might have ratified in early 1979 if only it had not been given the chance to wait until 1980 or 1981 or early 1982. The procedural tour de force provoked no publicized switchovers of conscience.

In sum, the extension of time voted for ratification of the ERA did change the rules at the eleventh hour and properly troubled some supporters and many opponents as procedurally unfair. But it was irrelevant to the final outcome. Opponents of the ERA seized on the procedural issue to reinforce their preexisting negative view of its merits. If the extension strategy also caused some supporters to lose their ardor, the strategy can hardly be held responsible for the loss of the amendment. Sponsors of the extension were choosing only between certain death in March 1979 and a reprieve until June 1982. Their procedural hanky-panky carried as costs some doubts about their purity, and some loss of support later for a fresh ERA. These must be viewed as negligible compared with the benefits for the ERA of continued life over the short term at least, and the preservation of a thirty-five–state head start in the campaign for constitutional immortality.

Renewal

After the extension period expired without the three additional
ratifications needed to write the equal rights amendment into the
Constitution, conflicting appraisals of strategies and tactics produced
different answers to "what now?" Some long-time activists let it be
known that the amendment might have succeeded had their advice
been followed and an earlier economic boycott of nonratifying states
been effected. Others regretted a failure to do battle against the
insurance industry which was believed to have lobbied against the
ERA in order to maintain allegedly discriminatory rates. Still others
thought a closer watch should have been kept on swing votes among
state legislators, some of whom defected—two North Carolina state
senators are given as examples—after first pledging support.[10] Those
who subscribed to one or another of these judgments looked to
immediate renewal of activity on behalf of an ERA—activity that
would focus on overcoming the particular failing they identified as
responsible for the unhappy outcome.

But many other sympathetic members of Congress and disap-
pointed leaders of women's groups, while evincing confidence in the
long-run future of the ERA, were uncomfortable with the ready
explanations for its loss and wanted to be confident of success before
starting again. In view of the strong campaign that had been waged for
ratification, they worried that failure could be interpreted as explicit
rejection of a national policy prohibiting sex discrimination. They
could neither afford to let that interpretation prevail nor afford to let
failure be piled atop failure. At the cost of some delay in the pursuit of
constitutional change, this group wanted to buy time for analysis and
reflection.

Although prolonged delay becomes indistinguishable from abandonment, equal rights supporters ostensibly differed only over when
and not over whether to renew the ERA. Those who argued on behalf
of immediate renewal pointed to the unique importance that the ERA
had acquired as a symbol of women's drive for equality, the publicity
that opponents had directed to its rejection, the substantial amount of

10. *Women's Political Times* (National Women's Political Caucus), vol. 7 (July
1982), p. 2.

money that had easily been raised by the National Organization for Women in the course of its all-out campaign for ratification, and the state and national lobbies still in place and available for work on behalf of renewal, if quickly mounted. Women and men who took this position were also likely to point out that available money and available troops only underscored what for them was a more important consideration of principle—they believed in the ERA as a matter of justice, and they were unwilling to set justice aside until the moment to pursue it seemed propitious.

On the other side of the argument, equally concerned and committed believers in equal rights for women found it pointless as well as "scary," as one of their leaders put it, to dedicate years of one's life to a "dead issue." And other leaders pointed to other women's causes neglected during the intense drive for the ERA that were badly in need of rejuvenation. The potential for immediate success in some of these neglected areas was deemed too important to overlook. Moreover, the argument went on, if there were no victories to show off, women would lose confidence in their organizations—apathy would replace enthusiasm.

To a significant extent, the different points of view about the future of the ERA that surfaced in 1982 after being suppressed during the preceding three or four years reflect differences between NOW and groups that felt squeezed by NOW's single-minded dedication to the ERA. Though NOW's strategy had provoked animosities, the appearance of a united front was obligatory while the ERA lived. With the ERA formally lost, both believers in judicial activism and abortion-rights proponents were especially anxious for breathing room to pursue their own techniques and causes. They had loyally followed NOW's lead on the ERA while there still was a live ERA. Was it not time for a shift in emphasis from a strategy that pursued pie in the sky to one that pursued tangible benefits that could be achieved? Should resources be funneled without pause into an ERA II that under the best of conditions demanded six to eight years of unrewarded effort: a year or two to move through Congress, another three or four years to move through the states—if that could be done at all—and, finally two more years before it became effective? There will again be a time for the ERA, said the skeptics, and while they were unwilling to pinpoint that time, they doubted it was the then-remaining two years of the Reagan administration.

Nor was the NOW leadership itself under any illusions about a renewal campaign that mirrored the original. If NOW's membership had soared beyond 210,000 during the ERA drive, and its financial intake for 1982 bid fair to approach $13 million, experienced activists predicted some fall-off once the excitement and promise of the last-ditch push for ratification was over. To begin again would mean having to do more with less.

In any event, the decision was to be in new hands. Eleanor Smeal's job was over. As president of NOW, Smeal had made the ERA her cause, but her second term, extended to allow her to stay through the ratification campaign, ended in December 1982. Her successor would be free gently to downgrade the ERA as Smeal had upgraded it. Any issue among several of indisputable importance could serve as surrogate. One, for example, that had come to attract increasing attention was a possible remedy for the "earnings gap"—a shorthand way of stating that women earn sixty cents for every dollar men earn. Not only would NOW not be disgraced if it stepped back from the ERA, and moved forward with the concept of comparable worth, it would put itself into the center of what Michael Evan Gold has termed the equal employment issue of the decade.[11]

The gloomiest evaluation of the political status of the women's cause argued against immediate renewal of the ERA and also argued against a campaign for comparable worth or any other important new measure or course of action. That evaluation found an unfortunate similarity between the success of the woman suffrage amendment in 1920 and the failure of the ERA in 1982 in that each represented the climax of a difficult campaign to which many women and some men had long dedicated energy and other political resources. That the one campaign was successful and the other unsuccessful was irrelevant. For present purposes, the relevant consideration was that ratification of woman suffrage ushered in no new string of victories. To the contrary, as Judith Hole and Ellen Levine have observed: "By 1920, so much energy had been expended in achieving the right to vote that the woman's movement virtually collapsed from exhaustion. . . . The woman's movement virtually died in 1920 and, with the exception of a few organizations, feminism was to lie dormant for forty years."[12]

11. *A Dialogue on Comparable Worth* (State School of Industrial and Labor Relations, Cornell University, 1983).
12. *Rebirth of Feminism* (Quadrangle, 1971), p. 14.

The woman's movement of 1982, far stronger than that of 1920, was not in imminent danger of death. But it was perilously close to collapse from exhaustion after the hectic pace of the previous fifteen years, particularly the years of the ERA ratification drive. Any proposal advanced without an intervening rest period would be hard put to stimulate a response from a large enough number of women to influence public policymakers. The bottom line of this analysis advised a "rest and recuperation break" before essaying any policy activity, whether for an equal rights amendment or alternatives to it.

Respectable arguments came from respected people on behalf of each of the three conceivable alternatives: to renew, to redirect, or to rest and rebuild. For a time, the behavior of ERA's congressional sponsors seemed to mirror the uncertainty of women's interest groups. The peculiarities of Congress's work schedule first made it appear that ERA's friends in Congress had decided to follow all three paths simultaneously. Emphatic declarations of intent from innumerable members on July 1, 1982, the day after the original proposal expired, presaged renewal—a ritualistic reintroduction of the ERA two weeks later.[13] And a ritual it was, complete with a ceremony on the Capitol steps attended by many of the fifty-one Senate and two hundred House sponsors. But legislation introduced in mid-July of an even-numbered year rests while Congress, in order to campaign for the November election, pushes to an August recess and the earliest possible adjournment date thereafter. Since sponsors really had no choice other than to delay for the ensuing six months any decision about whether to make a serious try for renewal, they appeared to side with both the advocates of renewal and those of rest.

Within a few months after the new Congress organized in 1983, old ERA stalwarts in both houses confused the scene with evidence that they might also have opted for redirection along with renewal and rest. Before any formal progress had been made on an ERA renewal beyond its designation as House Joint Resolution 1 of the Ninety-eighth Congress, proponents followed the leadership of Representative Patricia Schroeder in support of an economic equity act, itself a renewal of legislation proposed in 1981 by seven congresswomen. Schroeder anticipated the confusion about priorities likely to be

13. *Congressional Record,* daily edition (July 14, 1982), pp. H4063–85, S8168–79.

engendered by the introduction of the economic equity act. She
wanted to have it all:

> This legislative package corrects inequities in the law that hurt women's
> economic status. The inequities in private and public pensions, tax policy,
> child care, child support enforcement, insurance, and federal regulations all
> point out that women are profoundly affected by not having equal rights
> under the law in our Constitution. The economic equity act underscores
> the need for the equal rights amendment. The two are intertwined.[14]

Simultaneous advancement in Congress of as compelling a matter
as a constitutional amendment and as complex a matter as an
economic equity act that would alter federal law in five critical areas
comes hard. A dozen years earlier, Martha Griffiths knew better than
to try. She insisted then on according the ERA priority while politely
downgrading an earlier version of a women's equality act that "would
correct only particular, narrowly defined inequities, as opposed to the
broad scope of the proposed amendment to the Constitution."[15]
Schroeder's House colleagues got no comparable signal in 1983,
perhaps because the sponsor was herself feeling conflicting pressures.
On the one hand, "realistic" feminists believed the ERA unattainable
in 1983. To avoid the destructive consequences of another failure,
they would have accorded priority to the economic equity act and
contented themselves with just the reintroduction of the ERA. On the
other hand, feminists with an attachment to the Democratic party
believed the ERA, at the national level at least, to be a Democratic
issue that merited support on grounds both of principle and of
practical politics.

Despite the discussions about how to proceed, prompt renewal was
probably inevitable. Albeit a failure, the ratification drive had developed a scope and intensity not readily responsive to a command to
mark time or to redirect. Pensions, child care, child support, tax
policy, and insurance are areas of redirection important to numerous
women, but politically active women who had preached and believed
that there is no substitute for the ERA found its attraction both
dominant and irresistible. As for a rest-and-rebuild strategy, skeptics
questioned whether its tacit acknowledgment of impotence would not
be even more damaging than an outright defeat.

The case for inaction unraveled shortly after the new Congress

14. Ibid. (March 14, 1983), pp. H1145–46.
15. *Equal Rights for Men and Women, 1971,* House Hearings, p. 42.

convened when proponents could count 56 Senate and 238 House cosponsors of ERA II. Women's rights leaders who once gloomily predicted that it might take a decade to rebuild necessary support for passage instead found the outlook "extremely positive" for 1983. In early March the word went out that "major women's organizations and those supporting women's issues" urged a shift in strategy away from inaction and toward action on behalf of congressional renewal of the ERA in 1983–1984.[16] The amendment's principal Senate sponsor, Paul Tsongas, Democrat of Massachusetts, had already blocked out a schedule:

> I would only say that my own inclination is for the House to move first, that we should have this amendment passed out of the Senate sometime in 1984 so that people will have to be on record as to their views in that election year. If 1984 is the kind of year I think it is going to be, the state legislatures should then have the opportunity to ratify the ERA as quickly as possible and, hopefully, 1985 would be the year in which we finally put this issue to rest and get on with the rest of the business of this country, except this time with the full participation and equality of women.[17]

Because it is too big to ignore, because it is one of a very few issues that stir souls, because Democrats think it a winning cause that can only work to the advantage of their party and embarrass Republicans, and because it attracts a large cadre of supporters, the ERA resisted being sidetracked, either indefinitely or temporarily, after ratification failed. But those who view the ERA as the unfinished business of constitutional equality then accorded less respect than they should have to the unwritten rules for amending the Constitution. As a result, the halo around the proposal lost some of its glow.

Nonresponse

Translated from political language, Senator Tsongas's "inclination" for the House to move first on ERA II meant that despite its fifty-six cosponsors, the resolution probably could not achieve the necessary two-thirds vote in the Senate without the added interest and pressure likely to follow on favorable House action. Senate Joint Resolution

16. American Home Economics Association, "Public Policy Alert," March 4, 1983, p. 1.

17. *Congressional Record,* daily edition (January 26, 1983), pp. S533–34.

10, for one thing, had been consigned to the Judiciary Committee's subcommittee on the Constitution—an appropriate enough referral except that the subcommittee's chairman, Orrin Hatch, Republican of Utah, strongly opposed the amendment. That circumstance made sponsors doubt that the proposal would get a hearing, let alone the kind of logistical support that can facilitate favorable Senate action. Moreover, for the Republican-controlled Senate to pass ERA II would mean rejection of President Reagan's opposition to it. Paul Tsongas's inclination rested in part on a belief that by mid-1984 either the president would have forsaken reelection or increasing numbers of Republican senators would want to separate themselves from a president in trouble. The 1982 election gave Democrats gains in the House that were expected to worry the relatively large number of Senate Republicans whose terms expired in 1984.[18]

Senator Tsongas's inclination to wait for House action was perceptive, but Orrin Hatch read the same leaves and was in a position to control rather than simply respond to events. Why allow support for the ERA to snowball? Instead, if the ERA was impugned before the House acted, uncommitted senators might be won over to the committed opposition. Why not encourage a negative fallout from the Senate side rather than accept passively a positive fallout from the House side? Hatch scheduled an ERA hearing for May 26, three weeks before House hearings that did not open until June 15. Additional Senate hearings were to come later in June. In arranging for timely and adequate hearings on the proposed constitutional amendment, its leading Senate opponent thus appeared as a champion of orderly and fair procedures.

At the May hearing, when no Democratic member of the subcommittee appeared, and Tsongas turned out to be an unwary antagonist, Hatch found his enemy delivered into his hands. Within two hours, Hatch accomplished the near-destruction of the ERA— uncertainties and unanswered questions surrounded it, the proposal's principal Senate sponsor was discredited as uninformed about his proposal, and proponents were left with the need to prove that they

18. The terms of nineteen Republican and fourteen Democratic senators expired in 1984. Early that year, eight Republican seats were considered "highly vulnerable" or "vulnerable," while two Democratic seats were termed "vulnerable" and two more "potentially vulnerable." "The 1984 Elections," *Congressional Quarterly*, Special Report (February 25, 1984), p. 4.

were not being cavalier about amending the Constitution of the United States.

Hatch's assault on Tsongas was unusual and unexpected rather than unfair. The course of a congressional hearing typically involves an opening statement from the chairman about the importance of the subject, an invitation from him or her to other members of the subcommittee to comment, a prepared statement from the principal sponsor, a few courteous questions to the sponsor from one or two committee members, and then testimony from public witnesses who may be partisans or experts. Only under the most unusual circumstances will a member undertake to discredit a witness by vigorous cross-examination. The ostensible purpose of the hearing is to open the record to interested groups. It is not normally an adversary proceeding designed to embarrass or to downgrade anyone, least of all a fellow member of Congress.

But for this first substantive hearing on the ERA in over a decade, the chairman chose to ignore the unwritten rules of legislative behavior in favor of a legitimate-enough albeit surprise probe into the depth of the sponsor's understanding of his proposal. A series of questions from Hatch revealed Tsongas unprepared to discuss the ERA's effects on, inter alia, abortion rights, fair housing, women in the military, homosexual marriages, veterans' preference, seniority practices, insurance rate distinctions, and non-coeducational colleges. Tsongas's typical reply was that the courts would decide. Increasingly outraged by what he regarded a breach of courtesy, Tsongas eventually turned attacker, claiming that in fairness he should have been provided the questions in advance of the hearing. But Hatch blandly pointed out that non-senators are not afforded that privilege, and that Tsongas's long-time interest in the ERA should have given him ample opportunity to think through the questions raised.

The colloquy qualifies as an ERA disaster because it made opponents seem both more knowledgable about the subject than supporters and more concerned about what belongs in the Constitution. In fact, most of Hatch's questions had first been discussed in two classic legal analyses of the ERA—the leading rationale for it published in the *Yale Law Journal* in 1971,[19] and a reasonably stated criticism of it,

19. Barbara Brown and others, "The Equal Rights Amendment: A Constitutional Basis for Equal Rights for Women," *Yale Law Journal,* vol. 80 (April 1971), pp. 871–985.

published in 1980 by Hatch's fellow Utahan, Rex Lee, who was solicitor-general of the United States at the time of the Hatch-Tsongas altercation. Ironically, stripped of its pejorative implication, Lee's critique of the ERA on grounds that its vagueness and its uncertainty constitute "an open invitation, and indeed directive, to perpetual judicial policymaking"[20] served as Tsongas's response to Hatch's questions about specific effects.

The difference between the Lee-Hatch and the Tsongas position on the uncertain meaning of the ERA is the difference between deploring "judicial policymaking" as unalloyed liberalism and perceiving it as a routine fact of life in the American system. An appropriate response to Hatch's questions might have been that both sides understand the ERA to require judicial interpretation, that absence of detail is one of the glories of the Constitution, and that there is no cause to lack faith in the integrity of the judiciary. Instead, the amendment's chief sponsor allowed himself to appear uniquely uninformed about substantive aspects of the ERA, and to be goaded into responses ("We haven't got to unisex toilets yet, Mr. Chairman. Do you want to go into that?") that were intemperate or injudicious. His call for fairness, moreover, was made to seem a plea for special privilege.

One effect of Tsongas's performance was to invite anxiety among moderates about the ERA's unanticipated consequences. Another was to enhance receptivity to amendments that would expressly limit the reach of the ERA. Representative Henry Hyde, Republican of Illinois, the congressional bete noir of abortion-rights forces, urges an amendment barring use of the ERA "as a pro-abortion device." Because abortion is construed as a medical procedure performed only for women, Hyde explains, limiting access to it while maintaining access to procedures performed for both sexes or for men alone would be deemed a denial of equal rights on account of sex. Again, if sex became a suspect classification like race, Hyde believes government refusal to finance abortion would be akin to refusal to finance treatment of sickle-cell anemia, a condition that afflicts blacks but not whites. In Hyde's view, a proviso should be added to the ERA to make it abortion-neutral.

The linkage of the ERA to abortion, including forced public

---

20. Rex Lee, *A Lawyer Looks at the Equal Rights Amendment* (Brigham Young University Press, 1980), p. 89.

financing of abortion, that had plagued the latter years of the failed ERA's ratification drive in the states promised to plague the renewed ERA from its first day of consideration in Congress. Provided a forum and at least a backhand invitation to deflect the issue, Tsongas instead dodged away. Three weeks after the Senate hearing, the Supreme Court reaffirmed and extended its *Roe* v. *Wade* ruling that the Constitution bars nearly all state regulation of abortion.[21] Hyde's argument—which said, in effect, that an unamended ERA would eliminate the "nearly"—took on added importance. If that is what the ERA would mean for the abortion dispute, a majority of the Congress seemed unlikely to go along. If there was an alternate interpretation, why had Tsongas not made the case for it when invited to do so? Hyde's views had been afforded the benefits of exclusivity because ERA's sponsor seemed unwilling to face hard decisions about the meaning of his proposal. As a consequence, Hatch's hearing consti- tuted the sharpest setback to the ERA since President Reagan an- nounced his opposition to it.

Suspension: "The Process Is Awful"

Leading women's groups originally were undecided about whether any effort should be made to pass an ERA in Congress before 1985. Nevertheless, according to Tsongas's plan, Democratic sponsors of ERA II would let the proposal marinate in the House of Represen- tatives only through most of 1983 but pass it there before the end of the year so that the Republican Senate would have all of the second session of the Ninety-eighth Congress—up to the 1984 election—in which to temporize, and thereby alienate women voters. Given President Reagan's opposition to it, no one knew whether the amend- ment could attract a two-thirds vote in the Senate. By their votes, however, Republican senators either would isolate their president on a matter affecting more than half the voting population or they would stand behind their president and exacerbate an apparent disaffection of women from the Republican party.

Only a few months into 1983, ERA-now sentiment in the interest groups overwhelmed ERA-later sentiment. By March, those who

21. *Akron* v. *Akron Center for Reproductive Health, Inc.,* 103 S.Ct. 2481 (1983).

counseled immediate attention to state ERAs and indefinite delay at the national level had been overrun. The controlling argument said that without a big, highly visible cause there could not be a big, highly visible women's lobby. If the cause was put on hold, the lobby might expire and the cause never be resurrected. Moreover, were campaigns for state ERAs to fail—as they had earlier failed in New York, New Jersey, and Florida at crucial times—the national effort would be weakened if not discredited in Congress. Nine months after Senator Nancy Kassebaum suggested a careful determination of what went wrong for ERA I and how to correct it, the drive for ERA II bypassed the realities of retrospective analysis in favor of visions of prospective success. "The whole thing has turned from a wake to a new beginning," wrote Ellen Goodman, the feminist columnist.[22]

The new beginning barely survived the unwelcome exposure given it by Senator Hatch's hearing. Confident that he was ahead after the exchange with Tsongas, Hatch saw no immediate need to add to the ERA record. Instead, Hatch redeemed a year-old pledge by majority leader Howard H. Baker, Jr., Tennessee Republican, to schedule full-scale floor debate on a so-called human-life federalism amendment—a constitutional amendment to undo *Roe* v. *Wade* by reestablishing the status quo ante. The abortion debate that ensued constituted as much debate on the subject as most senators probably wanted. Defeated 50–49, the proposal failed to get a majority, let alone the necessary two-thirds.[23] But the count did presage success for an abortion-neutral addition to the ERA. Any such addition would be unacceptable to most ERA supporters. It began to look as if Republicans might have the chance to vote for an abortion-neutral ERA and to force Democrats to go on record against it.

Whatever symbolic benefit the Speaker of the House may have provided House sponsors of the ERA by designating their proposal House Joint Resolution 1 instead became a burden after Orrin Hatch seized the initiative on the Senate side and created trouble. Anything now done in support of the ERA in the House would appear defensive—as if meant to gloss over the mess Tsongas had made of things in the Senate. To do nothing in the House, however, left Tsongas's answers to Hatch's interrogation and Representative Hyde's testi-

---

22. *Washington Post,* June 11, 1983.
23. S.J. Res. 3, *Congressional Record,* daily edition (June 28, 1983), p. S9310.

mony on an ERA-abortion connection as the dominant commentaries on the meaning of the amendment. Since the former added up to "who knows?" and the latter asserted the ERA meant publicly financed abortions, House sponsors were in an awkward position; neither early action nor prolonged inaction by the House was clearly desirable.

Sponsors followed a modified version of their original strategy. They made no effort to accelerate House consideration of the ERA, or to call further attention to it before the last weeks of the session. In early November, the full House Judiciary Committee met in a long session to mark up the resolution. Nine amendments, several of them bearing on women in the military and on abortion, were offered and defeated, but ERA proponents came away persuaded that the opposition might very well have the votes to change those results on the House floor. If so, stalwarts would end up voting against the amended resolution. Its failure laid at their door, women's rights forces would have neither a legislative success nor an uncomplicated political issue to use in the subsequent election.

One or the other could be assured only by an up or down vote on the original language of the ERA, and only suspension of the House rules could assure an up or down vote on the original language. Representative Schroeder persuaded the Speaker that suspension was the course to take. The ERA, which owed it first passage in the House in 1970 to Martha Griffiths's success with the seldom-used discharge rule, depended this second time around on the use of another extraordinary procedure. But the procedures have contrasting purposes. The discharge rule is employed to allow a determined majority of the House to work its will on a bill. The suspension procedure is employed to preclude a majority, no matter how determined, from any action other than to defeat a proposal.

Consideration of the ERA under suspension had not been anticipated earlier in the session. In late June, despite the unforeseen setback on the Senate side, Don Edwards, chairman of the House Judiciary Subcommittee on Civil and Constitutional Rights to which the ERA was assigned, still agreed with a California constituent's preference for unrestricted House consideration. "Should the [ERA] legislation receive subcommittee or full committee approval," Edwards wrote, "we will bring it to the House floor under an open rule. I agree with you that any bill as important as the proposed constitutional amendment should have an open rule."[24] And Republican members of the Judiciary Committee claim they had been expressly promised an open rule making it possible "to consider two critical amendments"—one to make the ERA abortion-neutral, another to prevent women from being drafted and sent into combat. That promise, F. James Sensenbrenner, Republican of Wisconsin, has complained, took a "back seat to partisan politics."[25]

Whether or not an open rule had been promised, the opposition case is compelling. As Nicholas Longworth, Speaker from 1925 to 1931, once explained, suspension of the rules is "a trifle unfair" in that it both precludes amendments and limits debate to forty minutes.[26] Forty minutes gives short shrift to a proposed addition to the Constitution known to be controversial. The ERA had last been debated on the House floor a dozen years before its consideration in 1983. Not only had there been a substantial turnover of members, the issues in dispute—abortion and women in combat—had hardly surfaced as part of that earlier debate. Suspension is a procedure the Speaker is constrained to abide only in matters both meritorious and urgent, to use the solemn language of *Cannon's Procedure in the House of Representatives.*[27] However meritorious its sponsors may consider the ERA, Representative Dan Lungren, Republican of California, asks what case they can make for its urgency in November after the ERA had been allowed to languish in committee since the previous January: "Why did not House Joint Resolution 1 come to us on the second day of our session? If it so simple, if the words are so easy to interpret, if there can be no mistake about it, why did we have to go through the subcommittee and committee process? Why was there so much difficulty in the other body by the major proponents even explaining what it should mean?"[28]

Most proponents of the amendment chose not to try to defend the procedure. Don Edwards, who disliked it, insisted the fundamental question is not one of procedure but of support for or opposition to

24. Quoted by Representative Dan Lungren (Republican, California) in ibid. (November 15, 1983), p. H9851.

25. Ibid., p. H9850.

26. Quoted in *Cannon's Procedure in the House of Representatives,* 4th ed., H. Doc. 675, 78 Cong. 2 sess. (GPO, 1944), p. 403.

27. Ibid., p. 174.

28. *Congressional Record,* daily edition (November 15, 1983), p. H9851.

equality, that supporters of equality vote yes, opponents vote no, "and the American people will be watching." A host of others who also voted for the ERA nevertheless dissociate themselves from the suspension decision. One of them is Bill Frenzel, a Minnesota Republican who cosponsored both ERA I and ERA II as well as the time extension for ERA I. "The process is awful," says Frenzel.[29]

A defense of the procedure comes from Speaker Thomas P. O'Neill, Jr., Democrat of Massachusetts, who refers to the problem of the abortion and draft amendments and says there is no way the ERA would pass with either one of those amendments. Consideration under suspension is the only certain way to preclude amendments since even a proposal from the Rules Committee for a closed rule may be rejected by the House. If the ERA is not to be log-jammed, suspension becomes the required procedure. And, viewing it from another perspective after the suspension resolution came up six votes short of the required two-thirds majority, O'Neill would look at the *no* voters—109 Republicans and only 38 Democrats—and describe them as a "pretty good list of who is against women's rights."[30]

Even ardent supporters of an ERA feel discomfort over the way things were done in the Ninety-eighth Congress. They ask troublesome questions. Is equality to be achieved by the use of a procedural technique employed to stifle the rights of a legislative majority? If it is Republicans who are "against" women's rights and Democrats who are "for" them, should not the Democratic House have been able to produce the classic, lean language that its leaders insist alone suits an amendment to the Constitution. Were there not enough Democrats in the House? Is the passage of ERA II a partisan goal only to be achieved by such an unlikely turn of events as the election of a Congress in which liberal Democrats command an overwhelming majority?

Procedures Matter

The modern congressional politics of the ERA is a politics of extraordinary procedures. From Martha Griffiths's success with a

29. Ibid., pp. H9850, H9858.
30. *Washington Post,* November 16, 1983.

discharge petition in 1970, through Don Edwards's success in 1978 with a resolution to extend the period for ratification, to Patricia Schroeder's failure with suspension of the rules in 1983, a conviction that there was no practical option led proponents to avail themselves of some lesser-used alternatives to standard congressional practices. Only to the extent that the skillful use of an extraordinary procedure provoked no debate about fairness was use of the procedure a benefit to the ERA cause. Where the circumstances invited questions about fairness, the use of an extraordinary procedure not only had no positive payoff but ultimately weakened the cause. In matters having to do with the ERA, it would seem that tactics and strategies must not only be right, they must also look right.

Recall first the circumstances surrounding Griffiths's use in 1970 of a petition to discharge the Judiciary Committee. For twenty-two years its chairman had refused the ERA a hearing, a palpably unfair exercise of power on his part. On the other hand, the solicitation of signatures was carried out openly and with careful regard for conditions imposed by individual members—for example, Hale Boggs's willingness to be number two hundred and his unwillingness to let his name be used to bait others. No challenge could lie to the propriety of the petition; no justification for the opposition's intransigence came readily to mind. The ERA passed the House that year but was dropped after being amended by close vote in the Senate. The fair use of an extraordinary (discharge) procedure contributed to the push the proposal needed to pass both houses in the ensuing Congress.

After the initial optimism about ratification prospects turned to gloom, proponents reached for a procedure not only extraordinary but unprecedented. Extending the time within which to achieve ratification from seven years to ten years and three months was the sole practical alternative to certain defeat. Rational challenges were made to the fairness of the procedure. Unlike the earlier use of the discharge petition, extension led to complaints from respectable quarters about manipulation of the system by an oppressive majority willing to bend the Constitution to achieve a desired end. Extension could not have had a negative impact on the ERA during the thirty-nine additional months—without it, the amendment would only have died that much earlier. Extension did not help accomplish ratification, even to the extent of approval by a single additional state in the grace period. But proponents who judged the extraordinary (extension) procedure unfair found their enthusiasm sufficiently dampened that they pursued other interests when the ERA was renewed in 1983. In that respect, the costs of unfairness were simply delayed.

In the case of that initial effort to renew the ERA, there is doubt that the extraordinary procedure employed—suspension of the rules— was really the sole practical alternative available to sponsors. Suspension may have been the clearest safeguard against unwanted amendments, but unlike earlier circumstances that provoked use of the discharge petition and the extension resolution, in 1983 the life of the ERA did not depend on suspension. An informal head count indicated an ERA susceptible to floor amendments would be amended. In order, therefore, to debar a majority of the House from working its will, the use of suspension was decided on at a late hour. Fairness became a critical enough question for a dozen cosponsors of the ERA to defect, and for the otherwise pro-ERA *Washington Post* to endorse defections with an editorial—frequently cited by members of the House—entitled "ERA But Not This Way."[31]

Over a twelve-year span, ERA I failed of ratification in the states, and ERA II failed of passage in Congress. An equal rights amendment will continue to be proposed and, for the close future at least, seems likely to continue to fail. Breaking the impasse requires finding a way around the anxiety felt over the ERA's effects on abortion and women in combat or finding a way to achieve the ERA's purposes without an ERA.

Sponsors of the ERA could honestly claim for many years that they were denied a fair chance in Congress. But it ill becomes those once denied a fair chance to deny others their chance. Moreover, in the case of the ERA, it does not work. The evidence seems to show that procedural fairness counts.

31. Ibid., November 15, 1983.

Chapter Five

A Brighter Past Than Future

AT BOTH CONGRESSIONAL and state levels, ERA supporters confront different and more discouraging circumstances in the 1980s than those they faced in 1971–72 when the ERA first swept through Congress, or in 1978 when extension was voted. A review of the changed circumstances leads inexorably to the conclusion that the political fortunes of the equal rights amendment are in decline, weakened by the unpropitious escalation of disputes over military service and, especially, abortion.

In 1971 and 1972, most federal and many state legislators saw a vote for the ERA as an easy vote, a belated opportunity to show support for a proposal that had been suppressed arbitrarily for two decades by a committee chairman now in the twilight of his career, that had been but was no longer anathema to labor constituents, and that leaders of both parties endorsed. In 1978, a vote for extension foreclosed unpredictable new troubles. Had there then been no extension of the original seven-year period for ratification, two-thirds of each house of the ensuing Congress might have been disposed to start the whole process from scratch. But the easier, quicker, and obviously safer course was to take advantage of existing strength and vote an extension before the November 1978 election. No time would be lost between the original expiration date and the extension period. Debate could be circumscribed. Substantive aspects of an equal rights amendment need not be reopened for discussion. Matters of parliamentary law—Congress's authority to extend and the size of the majority required to effect extension—became the only subjects in dispute. Once accomplished, extension left proponents able to concentrate on the holdout states. The thirty-five states already in the fold stayed there, including the four where votes to rescind earlier ratification gave clear evidence of second thoughts about the ERA.[1] Extension

1. Rescission was voted by the legislatures of Nebraska (1973), Tennessee (1974), Idaho (1977), and Kentucky (1978).

was a positive-sum risk, its possible costs certainly overwhelmed by its possible benefits.

In the 1980s, many members of Congress came to see a vote to limit the ERA as a unique opportunity to register antiabortion views or to show understanding of their antiabortion constituents without actually casting either an anti-ERA or an antiabortion vote. For example, in 1983, James Sensenbrenner became a leading sponsor in the House Judiciary Committee of an abortion-neutral amendment to the ERA. That amendment lost in committee before the ERA lost on an up or down vote on the House floor, but an abortion-neutral amendment will continue to be offered when the ERA is considered under any rule permitting amendments. Sensenbrenner prefaces his explanation of "the ERA-abortion" connection with a reminder that he did not enter into the congressional debate on the ERA as an opponent, that as a member of the Wisconsin Assembly in 1972 he voted to ratify ERA I and also cosponsored a state ERA.[2] Like others, Sensenbrenner insists that his pro-ERA history not be allowed to trap him into endorsement of a constitutional right to abortion or to elimination of restrictions on federal financing of abortion.

If an unamended ERA does succeed in making its way through Congress again, the abortion dispute will be replayed in every state legislature that considers ratification. States where antiabortion sentiment is strong will be warned that ratification of an ERA connotes endorsement of a pro-choice policy. States where views about abortion are mixed will be urged not to back into support of the pro-choice position. Everywhere, consideration of the ERA will be affected by arguments from groups that insistently equate the ERA with both popular ratification of the *Roe* v. *Wade* decision and its extension to public financing of abortion for poor women. For example, according to a 1984 appeal from Phyllis Schlafly's Eagle Forum, "if the Equal Rights Amendment is ever passed, it will be a constitutional mandate for tax-funded abortions. 'Equality' is not really the issue, but an '*Easy Right* to *Abortion*' is! . . . There is no possible way you can be both pro-life and pro-ERA without an abortion-neutral amendment. . . . The only way we can preserve the Hyde Amendment [prohibiting the use of federal medicaid funds for abortion] is to STOP ERA."[3]

2. *Congressional Record,* daily edition (January 24, 1984), p. H101.
3. "1984 March for Life Program Journal" (Washington, D.C.), pp. 40–41.

Ratification, Chance, and the Abortion Dilemma

It is galling to proponents that by the spring of 1979 with better luck the equal rights amendment would have been ratified rather than rejected by very close votes in three additional states.[4] The proposal would then have become part of the Constitution before 1980 when its troubles multiplied. Technically still alive between 1980 and 1982, the ERA then faced growing opposition because of policy developments in connection with abortion and the draft, and the election of the first postwar president to oppose it outright. After June 30, 1982, with the record of favorable action by Congress and ratification by thirty-five states annulled, the task facing proponents took on an especially difficult character. The difference between accomplishing an ERA in the 1970s and accomplishing an ERA in the 1980s is the difference between topping off a thirty-eight story high-rise building and beginning construction again under a new building code after the collapse of a largely completed edifice.

The ERA flourished between 1971 and 1974 because the old liberal-labor opposition to it, grounded in support of protective labor legislation, reversed itself, while the new conservative opposition, grounded in opposition to abortion and to women in combat, had not yet solidified. With the window to enactment open wide and unobstructed by either procedural or substantive barriers, overwhelming majorities of members of House and Senate jumped through it in 1971–1972. The first three states to ratify—Hawaii, Delaware, and Nebraska—did so without recording a single dissenting vote. Eleven states ratified before the opposition vote in any state senate reached double digits. Among the sixty-five legislative bodies in the thirty-three states that ratified between March 1972 and February 1974, just six showed favorable pluralities smaller than ten votes, and only the Kentucky senate's twenty-to-eighteen count in June 1972 can be termed a squeaker.

But the only states that ratified after February 1974—North Dakota in February 1975, Indiana in January 1977—each did so by squeaker

4. *Equal Rights Amendment Extension,* Hearings before the Subcommittee on Civil and Constitutional Rights of the House Judiciary Committee, 95 Cong. 2 sess. (Government Printing Office, 1978), pp. 289–91.

votes. The initial slowdown in the pace of ratification—first visible in mid-1973 and more evident by early 1974—parallels both the emergence of interest in overcoming the Supreme Court's liberalization of the right to abortion, and the emergence of national admiration for Senator Sam Ervin as an interpreter and defender of the Constitution. As these factors pressed down on the once-open window to enactment of the ERA, votes for ratification became harder to push through. The close successes in North Dakota and Indiana—in both states, a shift of just two votes would have changed the results—indicate that outcomes were more uncertain than predictable in a middle period between the ERA's years of glory and its years of darkness.

Experienced politicians and lobbyists who take head counts before legislative votes can categorize the status of a bill as hopeless, assured, gaining strength, losing strength, or too close to call. In the latter circumstance, given the conflicting political and personal pressures brought to bear on them in dealing with controversial issues, many individual legislators do not themselves know how they will vote until the moment of decision arrives. Uncertain members come to decisions based on analyses that satisfy each of them. When all those decisions are made and reduced either to yea or nay on a legislative tally board, a normal distribution between the two is to be expected— an infinite number of votes by an infinite number of uncertain legislators will produce an equal number of yeas and nays.

As the fight for ratification of the ERA moved through the latter half of the 1970s, both sides intensified efforts to persuade uncertain legislators in the various states where ratification had neither been accomplished nor (unlike Alabama and Mississippi) been deemed hopeless. Divers votes on ratification were taken between 1975 and 1979, but serious attention focused on a half-dozen states—Illinois, North Dakota, Indiana, Florida, Nevada, and North Carolina. Illinois represents a unique case on two counts. First, a new Illinois constitution that came into force on July 1, 1971, introduced a three-fifths vote requirement for ratification of a constitutional amendment; without it, the vote for ratification of the ERA in the 1973–74 session would have been adequate. Second, votes on ratification in the Illinois legislature during the period under discussion were sometimes so entangled with crosscutting disputes over race and leadership as to make the ERA itself of only secondary or tertiary importance.

Setting Illinois aside, uncertain votes followed a normal distribution in the legislatures of the other five states where the fate of the ERA was finally decided. In North Dakota and in Indiana, just enough uncertain votes fell for ratification to pass the resolution. In 1975, the positive two-vote margin in North Dakota was balanced three weeks later by a three-vote loss in Nevada. In 1977, Indiana's two-vote approval was balanced by a two-vote rejection in North Carolina. In 1979, Florida rejected the ERA by two votes. Thus, in the five states where eleven marginal votes decided the issue, four votes favored ratification, seven opposed. As a result, two states ratified, three rejected.

A switch of seven votes—three in the Nevada senate, two in the North Carolina senate, two in the Florida senate—would have made the ERA the twenty-seventh amendment to the Constitution. While more than a routine break, a skewed distribution that put all eleven marginal votes on one side and thus added five rather than two states qualifies as less than wildly improbable. The two marginal votes in the North Dakota house and the two in the Indiana senate, after all, did fall on the side of ratification. Suppose even five of the remaining seven crucial votes had been cast for ratification, enough to put Nevada and North Carolina in the positive column by 1977. Odds then would have shifted in favor of winning the single remaining state. White House and other pressures on Florida legislators (and on Illinois legislators) would have intensified. It is a safe bet that many state politicians would find irresistible the temptation to achieve a footnote in the annals of constitutionalism by providing the final vote needed to effect constitutional change.

Even after the disappointing loss in Florida in May 1979, ERA supporters were not ready to surrender. Thanks to the ingenious extension arrangement, three years remained to win over three states. Afghanistan had not yet been invaded; women in combat did not occupy a prominent role in the debate over ratification of the amendment. Admittedly, the putative ERA-abortion connection seemed to have discouraged any forward movement toward ratification. But there was reason to hope for relief on that subject because the case for a connection depended primarily on an appropriations limitation that was itself under challenge in the courts. The ruling in that case could have a decisive influence on ratification votes.

The claimed connection between abortion and the ERA grew out of Congress's decision to limit or prohibit the expenditure of federal funds for abortion. (On the basic issue of the decriminalization of abortion, no ground would be gained by abortion opponents if the ERA was not ratified; the constitutional protection that *Roe* v. *Wade* provided most abortions would be unaffected.) Congress first enacted the restriction on medicaid appropriations in 1976, and battles over its wording in ensuing years invariably ended in more- rather than less-restrictive language.[5] The realistic possibility that ratification of the ERA would invalidate the limitation as a sex-based denial of equal protection constituted "the ERA-abortion connection." Logically enough from their point of view, abortion opponents enlisted in the fight against the ERA because it might ease access to abortion for women who could not avail themselves of it without public assistance. If, however, congressionally imposed limitations did not exist on the use of federal funds, ratification of the ERA could not be said to add any new right to abortion. The Court had already established a constitutional right to the procedure. Without the funding restriction, no connection between abortion and the ERA would exist that could be used as an argument against ratification of the ERA.

These "Hyde amendment" restrictions, which limited the use of federal funds for abortion, were challenged in federal court immediately upon initial congressional passage in 1976. Between August 1977 and September 1978 the subsequent trial produced a record containing over four hundred documentary and film exhibits and a transcript of more than five thousand pages. During the following fifteen months, ERA proponents remained hopeful that the "connection" would be destroyed by the outcome of the judicial proceedings. They were elated in January 1980 when a district court judgment invalidated all versions of the Hyde amendment on constitutional grounds.[6] If the federal government's appeal to the Supreme Court failed, the ERA-abortion connection would lose its rationale. While abortion opponents might choose also to oppose the ERA, they would not be able to claim that ratification would put the Hyde amendment in jeopardy and thereby affect the existing balance between pro-choice and antiabortion policy.

In February, the Supreme Court agreed to an accelerated appeal, yet

5. Roger H. Davidson, "Procedures and Politics in Congress," in Gilbert Y. Steiner, ed., *The Abortion Dispute and the American System* (Brookings Institution, 1983), p. 40.

6. *McRae* v. *Califano,* 491 F. Supp. 630 (E.D. N.Y. 1980).

declined to block interim enforcement of the decision invalidating Hyde, a declination that pro-choice and ERA supporters took to foreshadow an opinion sustaining the lower court. It did not. The period of euphoria that began with District Judge John Dooling's ruling in January ended on June 30 when the Supreme Court in *Harris* v. *McRae* overturned Dooling on a 5–4 vote.[7] By that vote, an arguable connection between the ERA and abortion was restored— with added respectability—to the usable stockpile of objections to an equal rights amendment.

The opinion of the Court in *McRae* held that due process does not confer a constitutional entitlement to subsidization of a constitutionally protected right—that is, that the Fifth Amendment protects the right to choose abortion but does not entitle a woman to a government subsidy to pay for it. It also confirmed that poverty, standing alone, is not a suspect (and therefore impermissible) classification. Ever since, ERA opponents and abortion opponents have viewed with incessant alarm the possibility that an equal rights amendment might be interpreted to confer the entitlement that due process alone does not confer, and that a constitutional amendment that makes gender a suspect classification would make poor women an especially suspect classification.

The ERA died formally on June 30, 1982, but exactly two years earlier *McRae* delivered it into the hands of its enemies. After *McRae,* because they could no longer assert the unconstitutionality of restrictions on spending for abortion, and because they did not want to deny that an ERA might supersede such restriction, many ERA supporters were backed into tacit acknowledgment of a possible ERA-abortion connection. Before the decision, they could insist that Hyde restrictions would surely fail the test of constitutionality, and that the alleged connection would be undermined. A contrary decision—Hyde formally confirmed by the Supreme Court—qualifies as a disaster for ERA's prospects and a boon to its opponents' prospects.

The effects were felt first in those state legislatures where last-ditch ratification votes were taken and lost in 1981 and 1982. Later, the invitation provided by *McRae* to exploit an ERA-abortion connection came to be used most effectively in a Senate Judiciary Committee hearing and in House floor discussion of ERA II. Whether perceived

7. 448 U.S. 297 (1980).

as a badge of honor or as an albatross, expansion of abortion rights is a heavier weight than the ERA seems able to carry.

Alternative Strategies

Public financing of abortion is to the ERA campaign of the modern era what protective labor legislation was to the ERA campaigns of the half century between 1923 and 1973—a limiting reservation that is a political impediment to enactment of constitutional change. In its time, each of the reservations turned some women into vociferous opponents of an ERA, cast doubt on the existence of a favorable consensus, and pushed ERA's congressional supporters to the use of extraordinary parliamentary techniques in order to assure a vote. The reservations do not have overlapping lives. Abortion was not an active public policy issue during the period that protective labor legislation intruded on the ERA, but that period ended at almost the same time that disputes arose over abortion policy. Consequently, there has hardly been a time when the ERA did not contend with the problem of a limiting reservation.

In 1983, supporters chose to abandon a tentative plan to sit quietly until 1985 at least before making another move. While adherence to that plan would have spared them some embarrassment, it would not have solved the ERA's principal political problem—the threat it poses to the balance between pro-choice and pro-life policy. President Reagan's stated opposition to the amendment made it convenient to view him as the political problem, and to assume that an ERA was foreclosed during most or all of his tenure. But it is even more plausible that whoever the president and whatever his or her views of an ERA, the reservation about its consequences for abortion policy precludes adoption of the amendment.

If there is to be an ERA, the abortion-policy reservation must first be overcome or neutralized. That it can be overcome appears un- likely. Proponents of the ERA, therefore, should be considering the relative merits of four different approaches to neutralizing the abor- tion reservation.

To wait. Even before there had been time carefully to analyze why ratification failed, the initial instinct of leaders of women's groups was to set the ERA aside and concentrate on election of more women to public office, especially at the state level. For example, NOW's Eleanor Smeal complained in June 1982 of a "stag club atmosphere" created by the lopsided majority of men in the state legislatures and said that the National Organization for Women would not seriously renew the ERA effort until a major change was accomplished in the composition of state legislatures.[8]

Although the reaction indicated a practical willingness to delay the fight until there is an atmosphere more conducive to success, it pinpointed male domination of state legislatures as the reason for failure. If, rather than male domination of state legislatures, it is the abortion connection that jeopardizes the ERA's prospects, women's groups might consider a comparable practical willingness to delay renewal for some reasonable period while the abortion dispute further diminishes in intensity. No one can expect abortion to disappear as a public issue, but only the most foolhardy ERA supporters will insist on giving antiabortion activists another chance to take credit for the defeat of an ERA. Ability to claim such credit adds to the political strength of the antiabortion cause, and a stronger antiabortion cause finds it easier to continue to defeat an ERA.

Hibernation can insure that the ERA will live to fight some other day. No one can be sure, however, of when that day will come—of just how long it may be before the political strength of antiabortion groups fades away in the face of more readily available, further improved, and universally utilized family-planning materials. Hibernation would be a careful, conservative strategy for ERA proponents to follow. But proponents who talk of "the legitimate demands of women for equality—not in another hundred years but now" understandably regard such strategy as one that promises too little, too late.

To fight. If antiabortion stalwarts insist that enough reason to justify defeat of the ERA is its negative consequences for limitations on public financing of abortion, then ERA supporters apparently must choose between denying that there are such consequences and acknowledging that the ERA would be an indirect way of overcoming them. This question of indirect consequences remains troublesome. Some politicians with strong antiabortion records deny that the ERA would in any way secure a right to abortion. For example, Represen-

8. *New York Times,* June 25 and 28, 1982.

tative Harold Volkmer, Democrat of Missouri, whose state did not ratify the ERA, says, "My prolife record is well known, and no one should mistake my support of ERA as endorsing in the slightest the killing of the unborn."[9] Volkmer quickly acknowledges, however, that other views on the subject hold that an ERA would wipe out the Hyde amendment and thus secure a right to federal financing of abortion.

The uncertainty only obtains as long as there is a Hyde amendment restricting the financing of abortion. Its inclusion in annual appropriations bills and the Supreme Court's decision to sustain it significantly weakened the ERA cause. While Hyde is on the books, it will be a reason for some federal and state legislators to oppose an ERA but no reason for any of them to support an ERA. Those whose abortion sentiments are pro-choice and who support ERA would be no less disposed to support the latter in the absence of a dispute over its effects on public financing of abortion. Some, like Harold Volkmer, who are antiabortion, are persuaded that an ERA will not affect the existing public-policy balance between antiabortion and pro-choice positions. But support for the ERA is weakened by the loss of an unknown number who adhere to what Volkmer refers to as "other views on the subject"—a belief that the ERA would destroy limitations on public financing of abortion. If the Hyde amendment did not exist, the way would be clear for this latter group to join or, as in the case of Wisconsin's James Sensenbrenner, to rejoin the ranks of ERA supporters.

A fight focused directly on the Hyde amendment thus becomes a plausible if long-shot strategy by which to accomplish adoption and ratification of ERA II. Without Hyde, the connection between ERA and abortion does not exist, and the extraordinary majorities necessary to achieve renewal of the ERA should become more likely. The Hyde proviso is well established, but some congressmen do not rate it impregnable. For example, although their principal goal is to make abortion available to poor women rather than to facilitate passage of an ERA, in 1984 two liberal members of the House, one a New York Republican, the other a California Democrat, formally proposed repeal of restrictions on medicaid financing of abortion. If ERA supporters made that symbolic gesture the point of departure from

9. *Congressional Record,* daily edition (November 15, 1983), p. H9864.

which to organize a congressional majority to confront and clear away
the abortion complication by repealing Hyde, federal and state legislators would be in the position their predecessors were in until 1976—
able to vote for or against the ERA without seeming simultaneously to
vote for or against public financing of abortion.

To compromise. If the ERA is ever considered under an open rule
in the House, and whenever it is next considered in the Senate, the
critical amendment to be offered to it is most likely to read, "Nothing
in this Article shall be construed to grant or secure any right relating to
abortion or the funding thereof." According to its sponsors, the
"abortion-neutral" reservation is meant to eliminate the possibility
that the traditionally worded ERA—couched in what House Speaker
O'Neill has described as the lean, spare language appropriate to the
Constitution—would jeopardize the constitutionality of the Hyde
amendment. Latter-day supporters of the ERA view the abortion-
neutral proposal much as their mid-century predecessors viewed the
Hayden rider ("The provisions of this article shall not be construed to
impair any rights, benefits, or exemptions now or hereafter conferred
by law upon persons of the female sex") to save protective labor
legislation. As preservation of protective legislation did not fit the
mind-set of most early ERA activists, neither does preservation of
limitations on abortion fit the mind-set of most modern ERA activists. And as adoption of the Hayden amendment then turned ERA
supporters away from their own cause, so now would adoption of an
abortion-neutral amendment.

The abortion-neutral language twice offends ERA activists—first,
by its theory that some impairment of equality of rights under the law
on account of sex is allowable, and second, by its nonneutral approach
to existing abortion rights. Rather than a proviso that the equal rights
amendment does not "grant or secure any right relating to abortion,"
a true abortion-neutral proviso would at least balance "grant or
secure" with "nor repeal or withdraw." While the latter form would
leave no basis for challenging *Roe* v. *Wade,* an amendment to the
Constitution that goes out of its way to deny only that it "grants or se-
cures" any right to abortion lends itself to interpretation as an implicit
overruling of the findings in *Roe* v. *Wade.*

An ERA can almost surely move through Congress again and
would have brighter prospects for ratification if its sponsors agreed to

almost any proviso limiting access to abortion. Federal financing of abortion under medicaid aside, pro-choice groups have won the abortion policy fight in Congress. Abortion opponents, despite President Reagan's support, found themselves unable to muster even a simple majority in a Republican Senate in support of a states' rights constitutional amendment on the subject.[10] And, while upholding Congress's right to ban medicaid financing of abortion, the Supreme Court otherwise has given little or no ground in the constitutional protection the *Roe* decision first accorded the procedure in 1973.[11] Consequently, antiabortion forces have little political bargaining power other than an ability to block the two-thirds congressional majority needed for resubmission of an ERA to the states. They would do well to trade that in for any opportunity to restrain abortion. But the costs of any such arrangement would be prohibitive for ERA proponents who see even less justice in compromising on abortion rights than on equal benefits under social security.

An ERA might have been enacted in the narrow period between the effective end of protective labor legislation and the beginning of disputes over the Supreme Court's liberalization of abortion policy. The best present evidence indicates that an ERA cannot soon be enacted without an abortion compromise. But a substantial majority of ERA supporters view any compromise as antithetical generally to the purpose and spirit of equal rights, and as an indefensible sellout of women dependent on medicaid in particular. This means that an ERA cannot soon be enacted with an abortion compromise because supporters will not agree to one. Constitutional equality for women in the form of an ERA may be sidetracked until developments in contraception make abortion obsolete and abortion policy irrelevant to any consideration of equality of rights between men and women.

To shift the battleground. In 1983, two-thirds of the House of Representatives would not agree to propose an ERA without a prior opportunity to vote on a reservation that would have preserved some

---

10. Reagan's position is most fully set forth in his essay, "Abortion and the Conscience of the Nation," in ibid. (June 28, 1983), pp. S9274–76.

11. "Since *Roe* was decided in February, 1973, the Court repeatedly and consistently has accepted and applied the basic principle that a woman has a fundamental right to make the highly personal choice whether or not to terminate her pregnancy." *Akron* v. *Akron Center for Reproductive Health, Inc.,* 103 S.Ct. 2481 at note 1 (1983).

restraints on abortion.[12] Even if two-thirds of the House had agreed, it
is unlikely that two-thirds of the Senate would have agreed. But if a
majority of House or Senate had added an abortion restraint to an
ERA, neither chamber would then have adopted the ERA by the
necessary two-thirds vote. Finally, if two-thirds of each body had
agreed on an ERA with or without an abortion restraint, either its
inclusion or its exclusion would have foreclosed ratification of the
proposal by the required thirty-eight states. Opponents of an ERA—
in 1972 hard to find and weak in influence—have shown that the
constitutional amendment process can be stopped both at a late and
an early stage.

The only chance to achieve an equal rights amendment under
present circumstances is to write into it the advantages that the status
quo seemingly gives to diverse interests that will not be abandoned by
their respective proponents. If such a constitutional amendment is the
only one that can be achieved, it is, paradoxically, a constitutional
amendment that nobody really wants—nor should want. The Constitution is a proper repository for a declaration of sexual equality, not
a proper repository for a simultaneous declaration that existing
inequalities may continue.

The American system offers a possible escape from the dilemma. In
1970, Martha Griffiths observed that there never was a time when
decisions of the Supreme Court could not have done everything the
ERA would do. In the mid-1980s, the observation qualifies as an
understatement. Decisions of the Supreme Court can now do everything an ERA would do and more. They alone can also bypass for as
long as necessary the questions that have created a stalemate in
congressional and state action on an ERA.

Consider, as the leading case in point, the congressional stalemate
over the impact of an ERA on abortion policy. Legislative procedure
and political reality leave no way for Congress to act on an ERA
without a prior vote to clarify its effect on government refusal to pay
for abortions. Although some members of the pro-life caucus are
willing to vote for both a clean ERA and the Hyde limitation on
medicaid-financed abortions, the latter is too likely to be jeopardized
by the former for hard-core Hyde supporters to allow separate votes.

12. *Congressional Record,* daily edition (November 15, 1983), p. H9865.

"For my own part," says Senator Jake Garn, Republican of Utah, "I am suspicious of the fact that those who claim there is no connection are the same people who strenuously resist amending the proposed amendment to say so." Hyde himself characterizes a vote for the ERA without the abortion-neutral amendment as a proabortion vote. "Vote as you wish," he tells House colleagues, "but don't assume you can have it both ways."[13] Ironically, antiabortion forces perceive a rejected or an appropriately amended ERA their best hope for maintaining or expanding limitations on abortion. No damage was done to that perception by a report of a March 1983 White House meeting at which Republican congresswomen who sought presidential neutrality on the ERA were said to have been invited to trade an ERA for making abortion illegal.[14]

These political and procedural problems might be bypassed in a renewed effort to have the Supreme Court declare sex a suspect classification in violation of the equal protection clause. Despite the political loss of the ERA, judicial success is entirely possible. As early as 1973, in *Frontiero* v. *Richardson,* a suspect classification finding by a plurality of the Court lacked only the fifth vote necessary to make it the supreme law of the land. Justice Powell in his concurring opinion referred to the pending ERA as a "compelling reason for deferring a general categorizing of sex classifications as invoking the strictest test of judicial scrutiny." The ERA is no longer pending. Principally because of the abortion complication, and to a lesser extent because of the military combat dispute, the ERA has been virtually frozen since 1976. But in other situations, as Lawrence M. Friedman has pointed out, with the status quo "frozen" and any movement deemed politically dangerous, the Court has done the "dirty work" that political or structural impediments debarred legislatures from doing.[15]

The dirty work only the Court can do is to establish sex as a suspect classification—meeting the principal objective of the ERA's sponsors—without mixing that ruling, at least for the time being, with consideration of its effects on either financing of abortions by medicaid or military combat, subjects on which it has previously ruled. In

13. Ibid. (February 7, 1984), p. S1093; (November 15, 1983), p. H9846.
14. *Washington Post,* May 3, 1983.
15. "The Conflict over Constitutional Legitimacy," in Steiner, *Abortion Dispute,* p. 21.

magisterial fashion, the Court can leave those questions for resolution in later cases. Congress cannot move again on an ERA that is ambiguous about them. A democracy should not have to work around its elected national and state representatives to assure half its population of equal rights under the law. But when politics and equality collide, a democratic government should take advantage of whatever mechanism it has to resolve the resulting paradox of an oppressed majority.

Index